A memoir of travel, grief, and an incandescent God

Stars Upside Down

Jennie Goutet

Copyright © 2016 by Jennie Goutet

All rights reserved.

This book or any portion thereof may not be reproduced or used in any manner whatsoever without the express written permission of the author except for the use of brief quotations in a book review.

Printed in the United States of America

First Printing, 2016

For my husband,
And for my children — the ones I have and the one I don't,
For Khadra,
And for Moguay — who now knows his Father

CONTENTS

1. Avignon — 1
2. Scenes From Childhood — 7
3. My First Call — 13
4. My Second Call — 21
5. The Valley Of The Shadow Of Death — 31
6. Flying — 38
7. My Third Call — 45
8. The Time I Answered — 56
9. Sober — 70
10. A Star-Studded Sky Upside Down — 81
11. Spinning Dizzily — 93
12. Chosen — 103
13. Sealed — 113
14. East Africa — 122
15. The Desert — 134
16. A Temperate Oasis — 145
17. The Fish And The Loaves — 157
18. The Year Of Weeping — 167
19. The Wall Of Jericho — 176
20. Motherhood — 184
21. Pause Button — 193
22. Small Concerns — 202
23. The Garden Of Eden — 210
24. A Surprise Gift — 216
25. Bleeding — 225
26. My Cup Overflows — 235

Epilogue — 243
A Letter To My Readers — 245
Acknowledgments — 247
About the Author — 249

My frame was not hidden from you when I was made in the secret place. When I was woven in the depths of the earth, your eyes saw my unformed body. All the days ordained for me were written in your book before one of them came to be. Psalm 139

1

AVIGNON

I was destined to take root in France. I know that now, even if I didn't know it back when I had the dream. This path was ordained for me as surely as my brown hair and green eyes, my ample flesh set on fine bones. My path was ordained for me as surely as yours was, even if it's just a whispered promise from a distant dream.

Of course it's only now, mid-journey, that everything starts to form a picture that resembles something—the rich-hued threads of identity woven together, the nearly forgotten events tied in tiny silk knots—all this has transformed itself into a tapestry, almost without my perceiving it.

My journey begins in Avignon on the bare fringes of adulthood. It seems fitting that my story would start in a place that was both the beginning of a path taken and the source of closure—the healing of a wound gouged out by grief. It wasn't with any set purpose that I returned to Provence in the time of my sadness, but our family's visit there collided in sharp contrast—who I had been with who I was now—the hope with the loss with the hope again. It was with this sense of heightened awareness that I walked down the broad cobblestone streets towards the Pope's palace in Avignon for the first time in twenty-three years.

I held off from taking pictures, confident that I would stumble upon that special square or shop or street that would unleash all the memories from a period I now regard as a turning point. I kept looking around for something to hold onto that would bring me full circle, but two decades soften the details. Time shrouds in foreignness what was once intimate.

I was nineteen when I landed on French soil for the first time, shedding everything that was familiar and comfortable once I stepped on the plane. In the strangeness that gave way to daily habit, I stepped off the city bus in the small town center of Montfavet and started walking towards the house I was staying in for those few months. I was alone, as my roommate, Jamie, had decided to linger in Avignon. The small nondescript square, which held the bus stop, led to the country road away from city traffic and bus fumes. I was grateful, for once, that I lived so far outside the city.

My surroundings were delightfully foreign. The pastures on the right where sheep grazed were quartered into small, green patches of grass by low-lying trees and tall bushes. The scent of burning leaves brought gentle notions of fall to my senses. A few large stone manors intermingled with more modern houses, the former set back on the hill and the latter bordering the street with thick cement fences. Just ahead on my left was a larger field with a straight row of tall trees, dividing the space in two. Breathing the crisp air on this deserted road was like breathing in the spirit of adventure.

After a twenty-minute walk, I reached the house. I turned into the tall, wrought-iron gates, left permanently open with their flaking white paint, and headed down the gravel path towards the back of the house. The dog bounded towards me, but he knew me by now.

When I walked around to the front of the house and opened the heavy wooden doors, I found the interior as still as a crypt. The floors, stairwell, and steps of the corridor, all made of grey stone, were cloaked in late afternoon shadows. I opened the door that led to the living room, whose threadbare oriental rug didn't completely cover the floor. No one was there. I then peered into the study on the other side of the corridor and saw the matriarch of eight children, sitting at her messy desk and staring straight ahead, lost in a cloud of smoke.

Jamie and I discovered that this woman had just lost her husband two months before our arrival, which explained her reserve in welcoming us. It seemed her tradition of taking foreign exchange students stemmed from financial necessity rather than desire. Why else would anyone invite strangers into their home so soon in the grieving process? But this coldness, this reserve, was hard on me. I had hoped for maternal warmth to help me through my first sojourn away from home.

My favorite season in all its hues coaxed me outside. I grabbed an apple and my camera and walked over to the shady path leading towards the bed of tall reeds. I took pictures of these straw-like plants, twice my height, then sat down on the bank, eating my apple and basking in the late autumn sun.

For a moment I forgot about the loneliness and strangeness that sometimes haunted me—the frigid bedroom my roommate and I shared and the midnight trips down the icy stone corridor to the bathroom. I forgot how much I missed my small upstate college and sorority and the large place I held in a small town.

The family I stayed with was an old, aristocratic family with every sort of heritage one could wish for, except money. The eldest three children were out of the house and one son was already married and living nearby. When he visited, rising with athletic grace and greeting me with a kiss on each cheek, I was too tongue-tied to talk to him. Two daughters attended high school and university while still living at home.

These girls were born with a poise I envied. They wore modest skirts, thin-knit navy or red cardigans, scarves around their necks, and their hair swept loosely back in a headband or chignon. The younger one smirked when I asked if it was safe to drink the water. But how can I blame her when I wore my naïveté so openly? The French keep their cards close to their chest.

They showed me how they danced "Le Rock," spinning each other effortlessly without music in their spacious salon. At night we sat around the tiny table in the kitchen, splitting a pizza four ways that would have served one person back home. We followed this with a green salad, bread and a modest cheese platter, and a piece of fruit. We rarely drank wine with our meals and were educated on the proper amount of cheese to serve ourselves from the cheese platter—not very much, that is.

After dinner, Jamie and I wound our way upstairs to the bedroom we shared. It was a drafty room with antique flowered wallpaper and a hodgepodge of paintings in mismatched frames, crowding the walls up to the tall ceilings. When we opened the long windows to pull the wooden shutters closed for the night, the cold air accosted us and made our dim room seem even more desolate. How different that was to today when I fling open the shutters in the brisk morning air as my husband and children leave for school and wave goodbye to them from our cozy home.

When Jamie and I talked in the evenings, I wasn't lonely—wasn't *as* lonely, I suppose. Our fingers were nearly numb with cold and we wore gloves indoors; or one of us would warm her hands on the bare light bulb of the desk lamp with twinkling irony. The remoteness and chill of our surroundings made us band together, but outside these moments of complicity, I often felt isolated by a fear and worry the other exchange students didn't seem to feel.

Why did I go to France in the first place if I was so fearful? And I am one of the most fearful people you can meet. Ever since I can remember, I have been terrified of everything outside my small life, haunted by the "what ifs," accosted by worry and the fear of dying or of grief.

But I had these grains of courage that propelled me towards France because the alternative was worse—the fear of not being good enough as I was. I was compelled to do something extraordinary to be worth something, to remake the old model that I knew to be deeply flawed.

I did recreate myself in France. When I sat outdoors on a stone bench, eating a baguette with butter and cheese and sharing a bottle of wine with friends, I was a bohemian. When I spoke in class with, what I considered to be, great fluency, I was an intellectual. When I met friends after school for a glass of wine at an outdoor café, I was a sophisticate. And when I took the train to Besançon and Montpellier by myself, I was an adventurer.

I was full of hope and the promise of becoming something

extraordinary as I walked the streets of Avignon. But it was in those hours alone in the stone house that I always came back to loneliness and fear. I came back to myself with a thud.

There was no lifelong dream of living in France that pushed me to step outside my comfort zone. I think I went because of the dream I had when I was seventeen.

I was walking through a forest hand in hand with someone. The trees made everything seem dark and shady, but I wasn't afraid. We walked for a bit before entering an open sunny space where we spotted a low, stone wall in front of us. We sat down on it, enjoying the day and the warmth of the sun.

Our conversation was intimate, and he said something, which made me laugh and turn to look at him. At that moment, I remember being surprised by two things: for one, I had grown into a woman, and two, the man I was talking to was French—and he was my husband. I was surprised to be so at ease with a man, much less one from another country.

So I found myself going to Avignon, feeling quite small, but determined to inject the necessary elements of change. There I discovered I had a gift for languages and that I was smart. There I got my first rush from traveling.

Oh, and I sunbathed topless on the beach in Cannes.

But all along, deep down inside, I think I was searching for that French husband of my dreams. And I'm guessing that's why I went to France.

For our struggle is not against flesh and blood, but against the rulers, against the authorities, against the powers of this dark world and against the spiritual forces of evil in the heavenly realms. Ephesians 6

2

SCENES FROM CHILDHOOD

You'll find nothing extraordinary in my childhood apart from those unique threads that make up the fibers of everyone's soul. My threads look something like this: daughter to a symphony musician and sibling to three others—one biologically related and two adopted—a renovated old house for our home, an emphasis on education, discipline, manners, and culture. Beyond that, my childhood memories seem to lack distinction.

My parents' story was pieced together from offhand comments dropped here and there. They both studied classical music at Indiana University, which is where they met and started dating. Apart from their common love of music, their childhoods differed wildly. My mother grew up in a wealthy part of Edina, Minnesota, the eldest child of a professional boxer-turned businessman and surrounded by a boisterous, extended family. She jumped into the family banter with ease, but at heart, she was a private person with a serious bent.

My father was raised by hard-working schoolteachers, and they stood no nonsense from their three sons. He bore the brunt of the discipline as the eldest and became a black sheep when he didn't fit into the mold of an obedient, religiously minded son. Though he made a point to be cheerful and hardworking around his parents, he got away with mischief where he could—like the day he went fishing after his parents forbid him to ride his bike to the farm. They drove up to confront him at the fishing hole just as he was swearing at the one that got away and an awful silence ensued—his parents too shocked and angry for words. When I heard these stories, I had trouble reconciling the image of a rebel with the serious man of few words that I knew.

So my parents brought this history into their marriage, its savor into our childhood. Without wishing to over-generalize, perceptions of the in-laws were such that one side of my family leaned towards teetotalling Baptist prudery while the other side engaged in pagan revelry. The shotgun wedding was a smashing success for everyone involved.

After having Jeff and me, my parents adopted another child six years later. Stephanie was brought over from Korea when she was just four months old. We flew to JFK where we met the social worker when she walked off the plane carrying two babies. She yelled, "Lawlis," and when we hurried over, handed us our baby. The ankle bracelet was the only link to show that she was ours. I remember thinking that the plane hadn't actually flown on our return trip, but had rather driven on the ground the whole way because I fell asleep before it took off.

When I was ten, we adopted one more child from a nearby city— my brother Mark, whose father was black and whose mother was white. He was born an addict from his mother's drug abuse during pregnancy and he spent the first four years of his life in a foster home. When he joined our family, he hid under furniture when people visited, obsessed over light switches, and set the toilet paper on fire. He shadowed my mother wherever she went. "Mark, I'm just going to the bathroom. Where did you think I was going?"

"I thought you were going bye-bye," my brother answered, still unsure of his permanency in our home. This plaintive confession tore at my mother's heart. Mark's borderline psychological problems hovered near the surface, and we alternated between worry at what would become of him and calm assurance that he would be okay. When it comes to family, you tend to make peace with the anomalies until they become the norm.

The inkling of a spiritual battle pierced the veneer of my somewhat sheltered childhood. I believed in God, and at rare moments, communicated with Him intimately. Yet I was frightened all the time. As a small child, I lay in bed at night, staring at the strange orange glow on the ceiling, trying to discern any small change in it. I was sure that I was witnessing the beginning of a fire and that we would soon be engulfed in flames. No longer able to quell my panic, I started to cry or call out to my long-suffering mother, getting louder so she would hear.

"What is it, Jennie," she sighed sleepily, standing in the shadow of the doorway or coming over to pat my head. "It's fine—there's no danger. Go back to sleep."

I was stuck on this periphery of war between good and evil, and I knew evil was trying to suck me in and steal my life. At the age of nine, I was waiting to cross a busy four-lane street with a friend when something compelled me to step into it. I knew it wasn't the right time to cross the street as cars were whizzing by, but I felt something push me. It was like there was this voice whispering in my ear, "Go. Cross the street. Now."

So I ran, with cars dodging me and honking, barely missing me until I made it to the other side of the street. My friend followed from a safe distance and when she caught up, scolded me. "Why did you do that? There were cars coming."

I just burst into tears because I couldn't understand why I had crossed the street against my own will. I also cried with relief because I had made it across safely. At times like these, I felt protected by God and could feel His presence. But it was only in moments of safety. In times of fear, I walked around the border of a yawning chasm in pitch dark, wondering at what moment I would miss my step and fall in.

I must have been about six or seven the first time I had a glimpse into the fact that I struggled with depression. We were still living in our old house, and I had just learned what the word "homesick" meant. I was standing outside in the bright sunlight, feeling lonely and empty. I kicked a tuft of grass with my foot and thought, *I feel homesick. But I'm home.*

At the time we were living in a poor section of town because that was all my parents could afford. I was oblivious to the fact and played happily on the mountain of junk in my friend's backyard, which held the thrilling attraction of an old car. But there was something unsettling about the place. The public pool had broken beer bottles, and I cut my foot to the bone when I jumped in. The babysitters were frightening when they yelled at me. The time we walked to school because the bus didn't come, some older boys followed us and threatened to set my hair on fire with a lighter. Jeff and I were mute from terror as we walked side-by-side, chased by their taunts and threats the whole way.

We moved into a better neighborhood when I was nine, and the new house felt like *The Chronicles of Narnia* with its walk-in closets and hiding spaces. I even pretended that by pushing through the coats in the deep closet, I would be able to enter a new land of magic. But my fingers touched the wall every time.

There were three floors, plus a basement full of nooks and crannies. We had a backyard, and what we called the "way back." Even the "way back" had a "way back" because the fence was broken, and we could run for a distance in a wooded area before seeing the backs of neighboring houses.

In the winter, we kids went outside after school to the "way back," which was set on a hill. There we navigated our sleds around the trees, laughing gleefully as we zipped over the snowy moguls before skidding to a halt against the fence at the bottom.

We stayed there until it was dark, sometimes lying quietly on our sleds, looking upwards at the black branches set against the purple sky, feeling the snowflakes settle softly on our faces. Eventually it started to get too quiet, too cold and dark, and we traipsed towards the house, my mother's face a beacon framed by the light of the kitchen window as she prepared dinner.

At the symphony, the concert began with the tuning 'A' as the discordant sounds of instruments playing independently fell obediently in tune with the principal violinist. We were at the concert hall often, sometimes as frequently as once a week, and I always felt privileged as we wound our way down the box seats after the symphony concert had concluded. We took the back stairwell with everyone else but opened the private door that accessed the backstage. There we found my father joking with the other brass players, showing us a side of him we rarely saw at home. Everyone called each other by their nicknames: Stevie, Brucie, Johnny, Dougie, Petey...do you think classical musicians are serious? They are not—at least not the brass.

I grew up. I was awkward, eating alone at school at a large table meant for eight because no one had invited me to theirs. I was cruel, scorning a love letter dropped into my locker by someone who was mentally handicapped, only to turn and see him watching me mock him. As I grew, my sensitivity to God and the spiritual world began to dull. I started to drink with friends when I was fifteen and look for modest ways to show that I was a separate entity from my family. The darkness that so used to terrify me became something attractive to toy with.

At sixteen, I was learning to drive in my boyfriend's car. There was a sharp curve in the road, and I wasn't turning the wheel fast enough to stay in my lane. At the last minute, my boyfriend grabbed the wheel of the car to jerk us back to our side of the road just as the oncoming driver lay on her horn in fear and anger. My apparent salvation barely registered through my flippancy. At sixteen, I was as invincible as every other teenager.

Still, at one time I was innocent. As a child, I whispered to Jesus at night, "Here. You can sleep on the pillow next to me," as my small hand softly patted the space I had made for Him. The thought that he would come filled my child's heart with an incredible joy and peace. And in the sometimes beautiful, sometimes wretched, long years since, I think that if there was anything worth redeeming in me, it was that innocent child, buried and forgotten.

From one man he made every nation of men, that they should inhabit the whole earth; and he determined the times set for them and the exact places where they should live. God did this so that men would seek him and perhaps reach out for him and find him, though he is not far from each one of us.
Acts 17

3

MY FIRST CALL

The first time I was nudged by God occurred when I was living far from home. It was one of those moves that, in hindsight, you know had to be divinely inspired. If I hadn't gone to that party in college, if I hadn't spoken to that particular person for the first time, if I hadn't been ready for just such an adventure at that juncture, my whole life would have taken a different path.

After graduating from college, I learned about a job offer in Southeast Asia and went after it. I had only remotely heard of Taiwan but discovered that it was a crowded, industrial island located parallel to Mainland China. I was hired to teach at one of the schools in Taichung, a largish city over three hours' drive from the capital city of Taipei. I suppose I went because I hadn't finished reinventing myself and felt I needed more sophistication. In any case, I was eager for adventure and couldn't imagine going straight for the job, marriage, and white picket fence. Plus, there wasn't anyone around who wanted to marry me.

When I walked through Customs into the dingy, crowded airport in Taipei, I anxiously scanned the hordes of people waiting to welcome the passengers. With relief, I spotted a Chinese woman holding a sign with the school logo and my name on it. I tried to ask her a few questions, but she patted my hand and said, "It's okay, it's okay." It took me awhile to figure out that she had no idea what I was saying.

I arrived in monsoon season. To get to Taichung, we had to take a bus from the airport to Taipei center, which took about forty-five minutes. A different bus would take us to our final destination nearly three hours later. This bus was located on the other side of a busy expressway.

That was when I found myself wading through knee-deep puddles in a thundering rain, dragging my year's supply of belongings up a steep set of stairs and over the bridge to get to the other side. Soaking wet, we arrived at the station just in time for our heavily air-conditioned three-hour bus ride to Taichung.

The Chinese woman handed me a can of syrupy sweet tea with chunks of seaweed jelly in it. As the exploratory sip assaulted my dehydrated, jet-lagged senses, I thought she was trying to be cruel, but her sincere demeanor told me otherwise. I leaned my head against the glass windowpane of the bus, watching the open scenery and the taillights zip by in the dark. I had never felt so exhausted, so alone, and in a world more immense than I could have imagined.

Eventually we arrived in Taichung at the house where the owner of the school lived, whose name was Bih Hua. She offered me some food and directed me to the shower, which revived me somewhat, but I immediately collapsed on the bed in the guest room with the door shut before she could bring me a fan. When I woke up in the middle of the night, I was drenched in sweat and couldn't get back to sleep.

Everything was so strange. The smells varied from one street corner to the next, from one footstep to the next—garbage, garlic, exhaust from the motorbikes, powdery incense smoking from a household temple. The air was warm and heavy, and there was a weight to the humidity that made me lethargic.

All around me I could hear nasal twangs as people spoke in loud voices in an incomprehensible tongue. I couldn't understand a single thing that was said, or read any of the colored plastic signs hanging over the shop doorways. There was no way to remain anonymous. At the time, few Westerners frequented this part of the city, and people pointed at me wherever I went, calling out "foreigner" in Chinese.

Even the children coming to the school for the first time would see my strange green eyes and turn away in fear, sobbing into the necks of their mothers.

My new house was situated in a small alley, in the middle of row houses with the back balconies nearly touching the next row of houses. There were clothes lines stretched across the railings with laundry hanging to dry. The air was filled with the noise of people who lived on top of one another—piano playing, meat sizzling in a pan, children playing, a loud voice. Privacy was dear.

I arrived in Taiwan three weeks before the other teachers, and though I could have remained with Bih Hua for those weeks, I insisted on moving into my new lodging to become independent as quickly as possible. She brought me to the house and opened the red metal gate. I followed her, pulling my suitcases in with me and looking around the covered, tiled entranceway. I was not reassured. There was a dead brown spider, the size of my hand, attached to the wall by one hairy leg. When I forced the humid door open, cockroaches and geckos headed for cover in a flurry of activity as light crept into the dark house.

It was frightening to sleep there all alone, and I unpacked all my things as the rain continued to pelt the corrugated roof outside. For the larger part of the weekend, I holed up in my air-conditioned bedroom, not even daring to spend any time downstairs because of the beasts. Only once did I gather the courage to venture out of the house, and to be on the safe side, carried my address written in Chinese. Sure enough, I got lost in those winding alleys and hailed an ever-present taxi to take me the two blocks back to my house.

Eventually the sun started to shine again, and my neighbor came over to visit. She chatted away easily and didn't seem at all perturbed that I understood nothing. Just as she was about to leave, my desperation for company took over, and I touched her arm then touched the door. She looked at me blankly. I pointed to the door again and made a sign of talking with my hand.

"Ah." Her eyes brightened. "*Mun.*" Door.

I repeated it. "*Mun.*" She corrected my tone, lifting her voice at the end of the word, which I parroted, and she nodded in satisfaction.

Then she looked around to name a few other things in the house, adding as she went to leave, "open door"—"*kai mun,*" and "shut door"—"*gwan mun.*" My first Chinese lesson.

When the other teachers arrived, I had this perverse need to show them how well adjusted I was, and I alienated them by shoving fresh litchis into their jet-lagged, dehydrated mouths. I hardly noticed their lack of enthusiasm—I was so happy and relieved finally to have human company in the small house.

My friendship with the other Americans was awkward. I combined bravado with arrogance as an unsuccessful cover for my insecurity. I threw myself into the things I was good at, like learning Chinese, but pulled away in the more complicated things, like relationships. I stayed home when my roommates went to the bar after work because I had formed a resolve not to drink anymore after my excess in college. This decision cut me out of the social scene in Taiwan and reinforced my solitude.

Despite there not being an immediate complicity with the others, it was only natural to band together to explore our new country. We went, timidly at first, to the strip of fast-food restaurants near the university where you could get soup and sweet tea, breaded or stir-fried meat, long narrow eggplant in a sweet garlicky sauce, cabbage with shrimp, green beans and calamari, green leafy vegetables with garlic, vegetables with bamboo slices and a chewy sort of fungus...Even by the end of my year-long stay, I hadn't managed to try everything.

We rode our new bicycles, complete with baskets and bells, and giggled at the scene we made as everyone turned to stare at the foreigners. In the city center at night, we saw streets of brightly lit stands selling cheap clothing or wooden trinkets and vats of bubbling liquid boasting chicken claws or wooden skewers with congealed pigs' blood mixed with sesame. By day we visited the stationery stores and discovered the novelty of transparent rice paper, colored pens, stickers, and scented paper with some nonsensical English phrase. We bought stamps and attached them with the help of a paintbrush and the small well of rice glue positioned on the table near the post office entrance.

Our neighbors and co-workers were kind and helpful. My assistant taught me Chinese, and I faithfully studied the vocabulary, written in my own phonetic code. A newlywed couple brought us to visit all the touristy places that bordered the city. We went walking in the mountains and climbed unsteadily over a rope bridge to cross the rushing river below. No matter how deep into nature we went, it was next to impossible to avoid coming across another soul as the mass of humanity spilled over every corner of land.

Not long after I arrived in Taiwan, my father called to tell me that he and my mother were getting a divorce. I still entertained a secret thought that everything at home would go on as it was while I would come back a new and improved creation, so this piece of news destabilized me. I cried all the time during those months, and although I tried to hide it from my roommates, it was clear to them I was unhappy. Without alcohol, I turned to sugar to escape from my feelings—the sweet milk teas, the airy bread with a sugary coconut filling, the chocolate bars at the local Seven Eleven—but that only added to the misery as I started to gain weight.

I decided to visit Seoul for my first required visa trip because I wanted to connect to my sister's birthplace. But I was afraid at having to travel alone and ended up spending all four days in my cheap hotel room eating cookies and pre-packaged sushi.

Three weeks later, I saw my roommates off for their visa trip to Hong Kong. On my way home from the bus stop, I stopped off at the closest corner store, whose shelves were dusty and half-empty. I carried my packages of stale cookies into the empty house and just ate and ate until I was sick. I couldn't cry, even though my emotions were raw—I was like a turtle whose shell had been ripped off, whose very essence was exposed and bleeding. I was so physically full and spiritually empty at the same time.

When Christmas came, I made the monumental decision to fly home, despite the expense. The thought of staying in Taiwan for the holidays seemed too bleak, especially with the turmoil that my family was undergoing without me.

I was no longer used to the freezing cold of upstate New York, and I couldn't seem to get warm. The two weeks went by in a blur before I found myself in Seoul, waiting for my flight to Taiwan. There I met a woman who was returning from her brother's funeral; he had committed suicide. She confided in me, the two of us sitting side by side, in the dusk that was starting to settle through the large windows overlooking the tarmac. I reflected on what a shock it must be to travel so far for such a miserable event, and my heart was moved by her grief.

Some things changed over time to lessen my loneliness. I rode on a moped with the Chinese teachers from the school to all sorts of themed teahouses, drinking the sweet bubble tea long before it was in vogue anywhere else. I began to understand nearly everything they said, and we had serious conversations along with playful ones. I learned who was having a baby out of wedlock, who was not able to marry her sweetheart because she had to care for her family, and who was arranged to be married to someone who was not a good man. With them, I didn't feel like a foreigner.

My relationship with the other American teachers had started to improve as well. I began to accompany them each weekend to The Pig-n-Whistle, the British pub on the other side of town where the rest of the expat community congregated. It was a relief to let my reserve down, even if it meant taking up drinking again.

One of the other Americans decided she wanted to see Singapore, so she accompanied me on my next visa trip. We took the cable car to Sentosa Island and lay on the vast, empty beach, looking at the cranes beginning their construction in the distance.

I swam in the shallow, blue water and lay dreaming on the pristine, white sand as I listened to the waves lap against the shore. On that quiet afternoon, I started to feel rooted for the first time since I left school. Perhaps I had a glimpse of a peace that was not based on comfort and familiarity but was based on something more solid, something internal. I suppose it also helped that I was lying on a beautiful beach with nothing to do but enjoy it.

As our year abroad drew to an end, we decided to go to Hawaii on the way home. In what was impeccable timing, we set foot on American soil in time to celebrate the fourth of July, and that night we lay on the deserted beach staring at the night sky as fireworks exploded in full color over the ocean.

While we were there, we stopped to watch a skit being performed on Waikiki beach. They were really good—funny, moving, talented. It was only at the end of the show that it became clear that the whole performance was about God.

In general, outward expressions of faith offended me, especially outward expressions of Christian faith. I'm not sure why this was so. Perhaps I just found the religion judgmental in spite of my own connection to it. I was furious as a sophomore in college when some of the freshmen on my floor came back from an off-campus gathering—where the subject was "God, Satan, and the Occult"—crying because the professor hinted they were not going to heaven. I went to the next speech he gave and listened with a set jaw. When it was over, I followed him and his groupies into the room reserved especially for people who had questions. I barely entered the room before spluttering, "How dare you tell people whether or not they're going to heaven? Who do you think you are?"

But these little skits on the beach in Hawaii were different. The people were talented, the dialogue was clever, and they spoke on the innocuous subject of love. When I finally realized what it was all about, I was impressed that such talented people would talk unashamedly about God.

Just as the applause was dying down, one of the actors jumped off the stage and singled me out in the crowd.

"Would you like to study the Bible?" she asked with a broad smile.

"Huh?" I blushed, startled. "Um…no, thank you," I finished with the ghost of a smile, and glanced at my friends who were starting to walk away. I quickly ran to catch up with them.

In my year of solitude and hopelessness, this was the first time I was invited to learn about God. This was the first time I was called.

For he will command his angels concerning you to guard you in all your ways; they will lift you up in their hands, so that you will not strike your foot against a stone. Psalm 91

4

MY SECOND CALL

I don't know how many tragedies I've been saved from—how many near misses I have escaped. I imagine it must be that way for each one of us, surrounded by that cloud of angels we cannot see, whose sole command is to guard us in all our ways, whose obedience to God is so absolute they hedge us in and close their eyes to the foolishness of our ways. *Are not all angels ministering spirits sent to serve those who will inherit salvation? - Hebrews 1:14*

I only know about the tragedies that have threatened me, but have not consumed me.

Upon leaving Taiwan, I needed to decide where to go next, and I'm not entirely sure what prompted me to choose New York City. I thought I might become an actress, thereby achieving fame—and hopefully with that—self-worth. Or at the very least, I'd climb another rung on that ladder of sophistication.

My friend Gideon from college was already living in Manhattan. She grew up near the city and had that hard edge I lacked. I was relieved to have a friend who was so knowledgeable about life in general, and especially about city life. I was feeling so green—as unsettled as I had felt when I first moved to Taiwan. I gratefully accepted her offer to stay at her apartment and slept on the foldout couch in the living room.

At the beginning, I spent a lot of time in Chinatown, more at ease in that world than I was in the fast pace of New York. Eventually, to put my own roots down, I left the Lower East Side and moved to Fifty-Seventh Street between Ninth and Tenth Avenues to what was once the Henry Hudson Hotel. This was a building of short-term rentals where people paid to share a room with a communal kitchen on one of the floors. Each room had industrial carpeting and old fixtures in the bathroom and windows, yet it was cozy and warm and there was enough closet space to unpack.

My first job was at The Gap on Herald Square, the largest in the world at the time. I wasn't making enough to live on, but I had money saved from my year in Taiwan. The people who worked there were native New Yorkers, and they had a hardness to their language I couldn't relate to and a bond between them I couldn't break into.

I spoke French and Chinese with the tourists every chance I could get. One day, two girls came to the counter with their purchases, speaking to one another in French. I greeted them with a "Bonjour" to show that I also spoke the language, although at the time, I was still more comfortable speaking Mandarin. They were delighted to meet someone local and invited me to join their group of friends going out for the evening. My social calendar was empty. Of course I agreed.

I met up with them that same night after work and fell in step with the taller male student of the group, named Olivier. Our conversation was both in French and English and was rather shy on both ends. It didn't take any effort for us to leap into a romantic relationship since both of us were interested and both of us were alone.

Soon after meeting Olivier, I quit my job at The Gap and started temping for Time Warner. I learned basic office skills there, but I wasn't sure if working in an office was adventurous enough for me. For someone as uprooted as I was, stability should have been the goal. But when I went to be interviewed for a full-time position, it was clear I was not ready to settle down to something permanent.

I spurned stability and instead took on two part-time restaurant jobs at night to make ends meet. The one on the Upper West Side was nearly always empty, and I soon left that post. I was also a cashier for a French bistro on Sixty-Fourth Street and Madison where everyone was scrambling to be somebody. Nearly all the hostesses and bartenders were models, and I felt short, stumpy, and uninteresting next to them.

The owner's son was there bar tending and learning the business. He lived off his father's success and expected everything to come easily to him, always doing the bare minimum. The wait staff was composed of actors or professional waiters from France who had taken up residence in NY, and the busboys were illegal immigrants from Mexico or Sri Lanka. I never saw such an accumulation of worldliness and glamour, of hanger-ons and under-world all in one place.

I met a man who claimed to know Robert Redford and who bragged that I need only mention his name to be received by the legendary figure. But I could see his insecurity as he stood at the bar, not knowing what to do with his hands. His words spoke one truth, and his body spoke another.

The hostess skimmed the guest list to see who had a reservation before coming over to sit at the bar and talk. For some hostesses, New York was just a brief stop in their lives, and they didn't take the whole scene seriously. "Can you believe some guy just gave me two hundred dollars to sit on his lap for ten minutes? Whatever. I'm saving up to be a vet."

But there were others who had nowhere else to go, and who were so clearly lacking in self-esteem, it was painful to listen to them talk. Michelle unknowingly revealed her emptiness with every word, remained silent when the rest of the staff picked away at her shallow vulnerability, and acted as if she were still young enough to get by on her looks. But you could see the panic underneath, the desperation in her dark eyes. At least for the time being, life had tossed her a precarious place with them. She was good with the older patrons, happy to flirt with them and feel wanted for a few moments, and that was all that was needed for the job.

The cash register was located at the bar, so I spent most of my time reading and talking to the bartenders when it was quiet. Once the owner's son seemed unusually distracted and quiet, so I asked, "What are you thinking about?"

He looked at me for a moment before going back to stocking glasses. "I had my first *ménage à trois* last night, and I keep thinking about how great it was."

People stole from the cash register and it was blamed on me, so I eventually quit. I had all these different jobs to make ends meet, but I didn't belong anywhere. I had a boyfriend, but I was starting to suspect he didn't feel as strongly about me as I did about him. I was surrounded by a whirling vortex of emptiness—or perhaps that was just what was inside.

About halfway through my year in New York, I got a full-time position as a receptionist with an up-and-coming wedding gown designer. Her warehouse was located behind Port Authority. This street was filled with homeless people and drug addicts who staggered by with needles in their back pocket. There was a brothel across from the office, and the madams and their clients did not always bother to take their business indoors.

Inside the office did not provide much respite. The salesman hated me and never failed to treat me to his cutting observations. I think I represented everything he detested—innocence, blind enthusiasm, young love, a desire to have a family. He lost no occasion to tear me down.

An older couple owned the office supply company in the building where we got our basic supplies. We could hear them screaming at each other from our office downstairs. One day there was an ambulance at the service entrance. The husband had gotten sick of his wife's ranting and threw a stapler at her head, causing her to go into convulsions. A few weeks later they were back at their dingy office, stacked high with boxes of supplies, a cautious peace established between them.

Things were coming to a head with Olivier as we fought about what would happen after our year together in New York. I had already decided to return to Taiwan for a year while he finished his studies. My year in New York lacked purpose, and far from having gained any sophistication, I ended up being more uprooted than ever. I figured that in Taiwan, at least I was improving my Chinese and living a life of adventure. I wanted to move to Paris after that, so we could continue to be together, but he didn't want me to come.

"That's too much of a commitment for me. I don't know if I view you as wife material. I view you—more like a sister," he finished clumsily. This precipitated my flight to West Virginia to stay with my mother where I cried for a week straight and tried to figure out where to go next.

Finally, he decided he missed me and agreed to my proposal. When my year in Taiwan was over, we would meet up in Paris while he completed his military service. In this way we also established a cautious peace—a trial period. I insisted on Paris because I was afraid to end the most important relationship I had ever had. But looking back at all that effort, I could have saved my breath. I was tenaciously trying to make it work, like a lone plant growing out of a rock, conscious that I had nowhere else to put my roots.

In spite of living in this glamorous city, working for a designer, and having an exotic French boyfriend, I still felt hollow. I was surprised that achieving these things didn't bring happiness in the way I imagined it would. My life reflected the emptiness as I binged on sugary foods and alcohol, and now coffee, working across the street from Cupcake Bakery. I was constantly trying to cope with anxiety and other emotions I didn't fully understand.

Ten days after I went to West Virginia to see my mother get remarried, I called in to work sick. I had an appointment at Planned Parenthood that morning for more birth control pills and felt lethargic, depressed, and nauseous from too much sugar. I was in such a fog I decided to take the entire day off.

After the doctor's visit, I began walking to Olivier's apartment a few blocks away. I couldn't bear the idea of going back to my empty room and spending the day alone, so I told him I was on my way. Lost in thought, I trudged across the street, barely noticing what was around me.

When I was about halfway across, a flash caught the corner of my eye, and I glanced up in time to see a yellow taxi whirling around the corner with the driver looking the other way. In that split second, my brain registered a stunned, *I'm going to be hit by a car.*

In the next split second, out of the depth of my decaying soul, I thought, *good*.

There was nothingness. A void.

BANG! The doors to the Emergency Room slammed against the wall as the first responders threw them open to wheel me through, the noise shattering my unconsciousness, images flickering in the dark like a fluorescent light sparking to life.

Then there was black.

I felt large scissors cutting through my jeans and sweater, jarring me into consciousness again, and I felt my clothes being removed as the doctors carefully placed a neck brace to immobilize my spine. I tried to make sense of the confusing sounds and distorted images around me.

There was a painful jab in my inner thigh, and I heard someone murmur, "We're testing for internal bleeding." Then I was out again.

I came to as they placed a catheter, and even though I was wrapped in blankets, I was still cold. I couldn't feel the weight of the blankets against my skin, and my body felt naked and eerily exposed, floating in the sterile, frigid air.

I know I kept up a stream of chatter, even though I don't remember what I said. I was too frightened to stay quiet. I gave them my boyfriend's phone number and told them not to call my father, as he would worry. But they did contact my family, of course, and reached my sister who called my parents in tears. No one knew how bad it was.

I slipped into unconsciousness again. When I woke up some time later, Olivier was next to me, and I tried hard to stay awake so he wouldn't get bored and leave. The doctors announced the good news every time another test or CAT scan result revealed no broken bones or obvious damage.

"You're very, very lucky," a doctor announced, to which I gave a little cheer. I thought if I were pleasant and upbeat I wouldn't be a burden to everyone, and they wouldn't leave me all alone.

Oh, but I was so tired. It was such an effort to *be* anything at all. When I forced my eyes open, the details of the room—everything—was far away as if I were looking at it all through a long tunnel. When I woke up again from another bout of unconsciousness, Olivier was gone. Night had fallen, and I was alone next to the beeping machines. I immediately slipped into darkness again.

DDDRRRING! The next morning, I was pulled reluctantly awake by the phone piercing through my deadened sleep. I didn't know how I got there. The ringing was so loud it hurt and I tried to reach over to the bedside to shut it off, but everything ached, and it was difficult to move. My head felt twice its size, and I could only feel half of it against the pillow. My limbs didn't seem to obey when I moved them.

Finally, I positioned myself slowly so I would be able to answer the phone if it rang again. A minute later, it did.

When I picked up the phone, I heard my mom say, "Oh, Jennie," in her familiar way that spoke volumes. She was crying.

"I'm okay, Mom. The doctors said everything is fine."

I was discharged that same morning. I was anxious to leave as soon as Olivier brought a spare set of clothes. But when I was checking out of the hospital, I kept wavering on my feet, staggering as if drunk.

"If you don't stop doing that, the doctors aren't going to let you leave," the nurse said. So I forced myself to stay upright by holding onto the wall.

I can't stay here, I thought. *If I don't take care of myself, no one else is going to do it. I have to pull it together.*

We made the slow climb up the five flights of stairs to Olivier's apartment. I puttered around mechanically in his space, trying to reclaim my life in comforting, reassuring routine. Sometime that day, in another attempt at normalcy, we had sex—surreal, unpleasant, and disjointed, with sensations on just one side of my head against the pillow.

On Monday, I went back to work. Everybody was surprised to see me back so soon, but it never occurred to me not to go. I was following all the usual motions and had no idea I was suffering from post-traumatic stress.

"I thought I told you to stuff the envelopes with the content facing out," my boss's husband said, as he pulled out letter after letter that had been stuffed the wrong way. I grew hot with shame. How could that happen? I know I stuffed them the right way. Was I not concentrating hard enough?

It took about a week before Olivier started to get annoyed with me too. "Stop acting up," he said. "You were able to stand up straight in the hospital when you set your mind to it. You weren't complaining about being in pain before, so why are you starting now?" The swelling in my head had started to go down, and I could feel my body again.

But he got a visible shock when I looked at the date and said, "Oh no—Olivier. I'm so sorry I forgot your birthday." I had forgotten every detail of having organized a surprise party for him.

Eventually it became clear that I needed to follow the hospital's advice and go see a neurologist about possible brain damage. He asked me to spell a word, which I was able to do. Then he asked me to spell it backwards. I just looked at him. I had no idea how to do that.

"Okay," he said. "Now I want you to count backwards, starting at one hundred."

"One hundred, ninety-nine, ninety-eight…" I paused. I couldn't remember what came next. That was as far as I got, although I remember thinking that if I started at ten I would be able to do it.

The doctor told me there was nothing to be done except wait. Although my mental faculties would return, some of my memories did not—both the memories surrounding the days before and after the accident and also certain memories from my past. The biggest change was that every childhood memory I had was now in black and white. The green grass of summer was gray; the walk to the public pool and the blue water was all gray. Memories emerged of people looking down at me from a child's vantage point with gray faces, black clothing, and somber expressions. There was no longer any color to my childhood or anything else that gave substance to who I was. My depression became more pronounced, and I was angry and defensive. People started to notice I had changed.

By now I had a roommate, and I generously lent her money at a time when I could least afford it. She disappeared without paying me back. I also lived in Olivier's apartment, while he was gone for the summer, to oversee the renters they had from France—renters who neglected to pay me because I said they could get to it when they wanted, and they saw an opportunity to exploit. They trashed the apartment and left. In all this, life seemed fragmented, and I couldn't make the right decisions to protect my interests. I was too distracted.

It was summer now, and I had quit my job in preparation for moving back to Taiwan. Finally there was a respite from those dark months spent in New York, and the remainder of my stay drifted along pleasantly as I visited New York as a sort of resident tourist. I drank black hazelnut coffee and ate blueberry muffins from Todaro Bros. I walked around the steamy streets of New York. And I lived.

One morning, I got up early and went to Bryant Park on Fortieth Street and Sixth Avenue. As I sat on a park bench, I saw in front of me a group of young people who were laughing and teasing each other with an enviable lightheartedness. I looked again and saw they were now praying together. I was shocked, and maybe a little impressed, because they all looked so normal to be doing something as singular as praying in public. In Manhattan.

Nevertheless, when the group broke from the prayer, one of the young women rollerbladed straight up to me and said, "Hi. I was wondering if you would be interested in coming to a church service?" She was nice, but seemed nervous talking to a stranger, and her smile didn't quite reach her eyes. I felt superior, condescending towards her. Perhaps I had some small degree of compassion because she was nervous.

"No, sorry." I replied.

She insisted gently. "Oh really? Are you sure? If you don't like the idea of church, we also have other smaller get-togethers…"

I shook my head again, my compassion now gone. "Sorry. I'm really not interested." I pressed my lips together and gave a polite smile, which effectively closed the discussion. I was thinking to myself, "What in the world? What kind of church is this where people actually invite you to go? They must want something from you."

This was my second call from God.

When you pass through the waters, I will be with you; and when you pass through the rivers, they will not sweep over you. When you walk through the fire, you will not be burned; the flames will not set you ablaze. Since you are precious and honored in my sight, and because I love you, I will give men in exchange for you, and people in exchange for your life. Isaiah 43

5

THE VALLEY OF THE SHADOW OF DEATH

I was more confident when I went back to Taiwan, having lived in two foreign countries and in Manhattan, able to speak two languages, and having a French boyfriend to whom I could write letters. I was also confident because everything was no longer completely new. I took the bus straight from the airport to Taichung on my own and directed the taxi driver in Chinese to where I would be staying. I exited the cab in the small alley with the red metal gates, and rang the bell of my old home.

The new team of teachers greeted me warmly and joked about my shoes, which were still polished, and my ability to speak English in complete sentences. I remembered how everything grew dusty over time—those new shoes and the ability to speak English naturally. I shared the house with two American teachers—Matt and Katie.

I was never confident having male friends. Either they were my conquest, were unattainable, or I was afraid I might accidentally fall in love with them. And who can live the rest of her life with a man who has ears that stick out? Or who dresses like that? Or has nose hair? It's only going to grow longer. I generally kept my distance with men, either out of insecurity or to protect my heart from a fatal mistake.

But I was comfortable with Matt. I knew I could be his friend because the boundaries had been set ahead of time. It was clear I had a boyfriend, so there was no ambiguity to our relationship.

I began teaching. In the mornings, the children peered out of the classroom to see when I was coming, and at the sight of me, jumped to their seats where they sat with their hands folded on their desks, as still as statues. I raised my eyebrow at them silently for a moment before we all dissolved into laughter.

This class was close to my heart. Their English was good after having gone to school all day for a few years, and I could branch out and teach other subjects. They said all sorts of cute things, like Emily's, "Teacher, I like your smell. I like your body."

Joey added, "Teacher when I grow up, I fink I marry you." I laughed and said I was much too old for him, but he looked at me seriously and said, "I grow big and I marry you."

During my first year in Taiwan, I had identical twins in my class named Catherine and Elaine. These two were sober, but I could see they were bright. After about two months of teaching them in my playful style, I sat down for story hour one day and saw them dart to sit at my right side and my left. I looked at them in surprise and was rewarded with the most beautiful grins. It was the first time I had ever seen them smile.

As I was leaving Taiwan that first year, their mother told me I had given her twins a precious gift. They had been born in a raging monsoon, with one baby pushed out quickly because the cord was entangled around her neck, and the other delivered by the mother, alone, after the staff had rushed out with the first. She gave them the Chinese names "Wind" and "Rain." But since they were girls, they were not given the same special treatment her son was given. The only ones who loved them and paid them any attention were their mother and maternal grandmother. The girls sensed this and hardly ever lit up with joy. But when these two came into my class, they blossomed under my smiling encouragement. I became close to that family and remained so during my second year there.

When I had this kind of success teaching, I was satisfied with my life and what I was doing. But it was not enough. I always felt like I was just biding my time until I could be with Olivier, even though he insisted I could only come to Paris if there was no talk of marriage. How easily those of us, desperate for love, can settle for such meager crumbs.

I went on my one obligatory visa trip to Hong Kong and stayed in the infamous, now condemned, Chungking Mansions—a firetrap that extended for a block, comprising hundreds of tiny rooms and housing thousands. If a fire broke out, there was no chance for escape, and I was nervously concerned for my safety the entire week I stayed there.

But it was cheap. The small, windowless room had only a single bed and a space to walk alongside it. The bathroom at the end contained a toilet with a showerhead above, and you had to remember to remove the toilet paper before you used it. I wanted to put my money into purchases so I compromised on the safety factor. I went to Stanley Market and bought all the Gap and Banana Republic cast-offs I could find before hitting every other shopping area. I remember sitting on a park bench, having spent all my money with two more days to kill and nothing to do. How wretched I was.

I had more than enough time to reflect on my mixed feelings. I wanted to be with Olivier, but knew that he didn't particularly want me there. He was young and completely focused on his career. I was living out the determination to have my own life, convinced that it was a necessity if I was ever going to be desirable to him.

One morning back in Taiwan, I got up early to walk in the university. I remember musing about strange things, thinking that if something were to happen to one of Olivier's family members, I would rush to be there for him, even if it meant breaking my contract in Taiwan. I wanted to be wherever he was and was dying for an excuse to go.

When I returned home, my roommate told me I needed to call my father back urgently. My heart sank, and I picked up the phone with trembling fingers. I knew nothing good could come out of this call.

"Mark committed suicide," my father said, speaking of my brother. "He shot himself with my hunting gun. He'd been accused of stealing the neighbor's heirloom rings and was brought to the police station and booked. They let him come home because they had no solid evidence to keep him."

My father's voice was choked with emotion as he continued. "I could see that he was really upset, and I told him that no matter what happened, I would be there for him. I told him that I loved him." He cleared his throat and went on, "But when I came home from running errands, I found him."

I was silent. My face was hot and my hands were cold. My heart was beating fast, and I couldn't process the reality because of the roaring in my ears. "How's Mom? How are Jeff and Stephanie?" I asked. I couldn't bear to ask myself, "How are *you*?"

We said other meaningless words—words that could only dance around the tragedy and not address it. I said I would try to think about coming home, but the thought of planning a trip was so overwhelming I didn't know how to proceed. When I opened the door, Matt was standing there, his face stricken.

"My brother committed suicide," I said. He wanted to fold me into his arms, but I moved forward numbly to sit in the living room, my face betraying nothing.

I didn't think about going home straight away, but after a day or two, I had made my decision. It was right after the New Year, and not easy to get a plane reservation or bus ticket to the airport, but a friend found one for me through a private company. Before dawn, my friend Jill took me on her moped forty-five minutes away, my huge suitcase at her feet. From there I took the cramped, private van to the airport.

The first leg of the flight was to Tokyo, four and a half hours away. After just two hours, the pilot announced there was engine trouble and that it was closer to turn back, so we were flying back to Taipei. We waited a few hours on the tarmac while they fixed the problem before taking off again.

When we arrived in Tokyo, those of us taking the connecting flight had to rush to get it. I had gotten my ticket last minute, so I was in the middle seat against the toilets. My seat did not recline.

I was also the last one to board and there was no more room for my carry-on, so I had to shove my small suitcase between my legs. Next to me sat a pregnant woman, and on the other side an older, somewhat loud Cantonese-speaking couple. I sat unmoving, without sleeping, staring at the spotlight on my foldout table for thirteen hours.

When I got to Detroit, they announced the baggage conveyor belt was broken. We waited while they brought our luggage out by hand so we could carry it through customs. I stood for over an hour with exhaustion, grief, and shock vying for domination over my psyche and finally headed over to another terminal for the last leg to Syracuse.

When I got to the gate, they announced the flight might not take off because there was a blizzard in Syracuse. Eventually the plane did take off and touched down in a hair-raising landing, skidding to the right and left, the wings almost scraping the runway as we bounced to a stop.

My mother and her husband picked me up to take me to his friends' house to spend the night. But our car broke down on the way, and we had to stop at a repair shop and wait in the cold for it to be fixed. I finally fell asleep in a strange bed over thirty hours after I had first started my journey, my heart troubled to the point of death.

The funeral was grisly. Symphony friends played Albinoni's "Adagio in G Minor." My father spoke, I spoke. I don't remember what I said, but I remember feeling like I didn't take a single breath the entire speech. I don't remember how each member of my family grieved; we just walked around in our own orbit of misery. I could barely stand from fatigue and grief as I accepted everyone's condolences.

After the funeral, my dad and I went to the place where it happened. There was a record-breaking cold spell in upstate New York. The bitter cold was even more unbearable having come from tropical Taiwan. The cold settled in my bones and chilled my heart as if the spirit world had been unleashed and was winding its tentacles around me.

I followed my father into his apartment. He was renting the bottom floor of the house next to the one I grew up in, so out the window I could see someone else's Christmas decorations still sitting on the porch where the four of us used to run from column to column. The heat was off and boxes of storage lined the wall. The rooms were white, sterile, and nearly as cold as the outdoors. As I stood looking around at the empty walls, my father described what happened:

"I came into the kitchen and immediately noticed a strange smell. I turned the corner into the pantry and saw something on the wall in the living room, but I didn't know what it was. I stood there, shocked, looking around, thinking, 'The place has been vandalized.' And then I thought, 'Could Mark have done this since he had been so be upset?' There were dark stains all over the living room wall, and at my feet there was what looked like a piece of melted candle."

"Then I saw his feet extended from the edge of the bed in my bedroom, and it dawned on me that what I saw on the floor was part of his skull. It was at that moment that I realized he must have shot himself. I wanted to hug him but I knew he was gone, and there was nothing I could do. I called 911 and sat down on the sofa, crying, while I waited for help to come."

When my father was done speaking, I felt like acid coursed through my veins. I went numbly into the bathroom where I lay down on the tiled floor, curled up in a ball next to the toilet. The pipes underneath leaked brown rust onto the white porcelain. I was so cold and so dead inside. I thought, *I will never feel joy again. I will never feel love again. I won't feel anything at all.*

Your wrath has swept over me; your terrors have destroyed me. All day long they surround me like a flood; they have completely engulfed me. You have taken my companions and loved ones from me; the darkness is my closest friend. Psalm 88

6

FLYING

I had to go back, and oh God how I didn't want to. But when you grieve, life winds its cords around you and carries you off, whether or not you are willing.

I took the train into Manhattan where I met with Olivier for a few days before flying out. He was back from France after the holidays—in part to support me but mainly to tie up loose ends before moving back to France. He listened to me attempt to express some of the horror but didn't ask any questions. His relief was palpable when the topic moved on to other things, and he quickly turned his attention to soaking up as much of the city as he could before moving on to the next stage of his life.

I flew back to Taiwan alone, and while on layover in Seoul, remembered the woman who had flown back to Asia after attending her brother's funeral—the woman whose brother had committed suicide. The ghost of our conversation superimposed over my reality, her sorrow over my sorrow, as I sat there in the nearly empty terminal.

When I walked into the school for the first time after two weeks, the entire schoolyard of small children and teachers erupted in cheers. This was not the reaction I wanted or needed, and I had to turn back outside to control my tears and anger. I was angry that people thought

I would be ready to move on with my life so soon. I was angry that they were happy to see me, that their lives were continuing gaily when this horrible loss had turned mine upside down.

I had changed again. Whatever positive changes I had embraced to heal and grow stronger following the car accident were thrust aside as I was hurled down by my grief. Everyone noticed how negative and defensive I had become, and I permanently alienated many of my friends.

In those winter months—the bearable season in tropical Taiwan—I spent a lot of time alone. I had terrible nightmares. Sometimes I woke up so terrified I could see the veins in my chest pulsing underneath my skin because my heart was beating so fast. I had this constant sense of foreboding, a feeling that often jolted me out of a deep sleep and left me gasping for breath.

The thought of eating meat repulsed me for the first time, and I became a vegetarian until I moved to France. Matt took me on his motorcycle to the vegetarian Buddhist stand in a market a little further from our usual haunt. We sat at the crowded outdoor tables, eating a wide variety of delicious tofu dishes. With him, at least, I could have easy conversation. He was always able to match my mood—reckless, despondent, falsely gay, meditative. He was always attuned to what I needed.

My students wanted to know what happened. They asked questions which I couldn't answer and which evoked haunting visions that momentarily staggered me. They didn't understand this shadow of a teacher who never smiled anymore. Ada, my Chinese Assistant, worried about the wrinkle that was developing in the middle of my forehead and smoothed the skin with her thumbs to try and take away my wrinkles—and with them, my worries. She soothed me with her affection but could not reach me in my emotional isolation.

One night I had a dream. Oh, it was such a vivid, *real* dream. I was at the top of a tall tower and all around me were glass windows overlooking a city at night. The sky was pitch black, and I could hear loud, threatening explosions. When I peered out the window, I saw bombs exploding below me, lighting up the dark streets and the horizon. I was alert and knew that I was in danger. I had to get out. I had to find a way to enter the war zone, as impossible as that seemed, and find a safe place to hide.

Something caught my attention out of the corner of my eye, and I looked over to my side and saw Mark—my brother Mark. He was real! He was right there! I grabbed him and clung to him, so overjoyed to see him again. I almost felt like I could keep him with me simply by the force of my will but somehow even in my dream I knew he would have to leave.

I asked him, "What's it like there?" We both knew I was talking about the afterlife. He shook his head and hesitated, before saying, "Scary."

That silenced me for a moment and I looked down. I felt it in my soul that he must be right. It had to be awful and scary because I was already filled with dread from the war that was going on where I was.

I took him by the arm and said, "You have to come with me. You have to come and visit Dad because he misses you so much." All the longing of my heart poured into my words and my urging. I wanted to erase the last vision my father had of him and fill the terrible hole that was left in my family. I knew my brother was the missing element that could make everything right again.

Mark shook his head slightly at my words, but he came with me into the elevator just the same. We started the long descent to the bottom together, staring straight ahead. My shoulders slumped as it dawned on me that there were no more words to be said between us.

In the last instant before we arrived on the ground floor, I turned to look at Mark, and he was gone. Suddenly, the sound of an explosion rocked me sideways off my feet. My eyes flew open and I found myself in my own room, sitting upright in bed, with the sound of firecrackers skittering along the alley outside my window.

It was Chinese New Year.

The first year I lived in Taiwan, one of the teachers convinced me to go to church with her. It was a forty-five-minute bicycle ride away, and we were the only two American teachers interested in going. When I returned to Taiwan, I continued going from time to time by myself because I liked seeing other Westerners there. I suppose I also went because I thought it was the right thing to do.

I can't really say I was seeking God. I don't remember ever praying or thinking about Him outside of those brief church services. After Mark died, it didn't occur to me to pray even once. In the personal hell I was dwelling in, God was nowhere to be found.

The first time I attended church after Mark died, I sat in the back of the tiny sanctuary away from the prying eyes of people I didn't know. My heart was so raw I cried the entire service. When it was over, the girl sitting in my pew, who was about my age, asked with concern if she could help. Her name was Coralie.

I tried to keep it together as I told her about my brother's suicide, my words caught in my throat as I tried to control my emotions. She listened with a grave expression, her eyes full of compassion for my naked grief.

When I finished speaking, she said hesitatingly, "There's a Christian psychologist who is doing mission work here in Taiwan for a few months. He goes to the church over at the American school." She paused to judge my reaction. "If you want, I can put you in touch with him—if you think it might help to talk to someone."

I nodded my assent and whispered, "Okay."

The first time I went to see this psychologist was over my lunch break. I was mortified at the thought that someone might find out, so I tried to think of some excuse for where I was going in case another teacher asked. "I'm going to meet a friend for lunch who works over on the other side of town," I practiced in my head.

It was hard to open up. I wasn't used to counseling and didn't know where to begin. I saw him for a few months before his mission ended and he went back to the States. I don't remember much about our sessions other than the kindness with which he embraced the outpouring of my venomous pain, but I do remember him giving me a Bible during our last session with a passage highlighted in it. It was Philippians 1:3-6.

I thank my God every time I remember you. In all my prayers for all of you, I always pray with joy because of your partnership in the gospel from the first day until now, being confident of this, that he who began a good work in you will carry it on to completion until the day of Christ Jesus.

We read the passage together and he said, "I have been praying for you, and I will keep praying for you. I'm confident that God has begun a good work in you that He will carry on to completion."

I couldn't grasp the concept that someone I barely knew was praying for me. Why would he even care about me enough to do that? But I was touched. I was also astonished at how easy it was to read the Bible and how directly it spoke to my heart. So I began to read this Bible from time to time, curious about the things I read.

Coralie proved herself a true friend and came to spend time with me once a week, riding her motorcycle an hour each way, sometimes in the pouring rain. At times I asked her to explain something I had read in the Bible. I had many prejudices against religion and against God, and she answered me with a humility I have never been able to acquire. When I asked her how God could let cruel things happen, she answered in her soft Australian accent, "I don't know much. I don't know how to answer you. But I know that God is good."

My heart was softened by her love, and I found that I didn't mind if she didn't have answers. Her humility was a perfect match for my pride because I had no one to fight against. Something resembling faith started to penetrate my heart.

My beloved class at school was taken away from me as all my students left to go to Chinese public school fulltime. I was given an entirely new class that was rowdy and twice as large, which met in the small, communal space shared by the other classes. I began to get desperate, counting down the days until I could leave and go to Paris. I tried to push away the thought that without my class I didn't belong in Taiwan anymore; without Olivier's wholehearted welcome, I didn't belong in Paris; and without my family intact, I didn't belong in New York. It seemed I didn't belong anywhere.

My old Teaching Assistant, Elva, was still in my life, although she had moved to Taipei. One weekend she visited and took me into the mountains. I loved riding the motorbike. I felt so free, whipping past the people and the sights at an exhilarating pace. Helmets were not required, and I didn't care whether or not I survived a fall, so I let the wind tug at my hair freely and brace against my body. I wanted the wind to rip the pain out of my chest.

At first we drove through the familiar busy streets, loud vendors pushing their wares at every turn. We stopped at the lights, lost in an army of motorbikes, the thick white clouds of exhaust reaching up to the first story of the buildings nearby. Then the roadways opened up and became larger as we saw more and more of the countryside. We rode on for over an hour like that and then, there in the distance—the mountains.

We drove onto the straight, wide road that crossed the rice paddies on either side and eventually wound its way up the mountain. The curves in the road pulled our bodies to one side and the other as we climbed our way to the top. We found a little dirt semicircle off the side of the road to park, and as soon as we switched off the motor, I noticed how still it was. No one was there but us.

Baskets in hand, we began to pick the wild litchis in the tall bushes, reaching higher and higher to get the largest, juiciest ones above our heads. We stopped to peel the purple cardboard skin of the fruit and taste its cloying sweetness, before spitting out the smooth brown pit, our fingers sticky with juice. When we had filled our baskets, we returned to the road and drove until we found the large stream winding its way down the mountain. In the center were two broad, flat rocks that jutted out of the rushing stream of water, beckoning us to come sit.

Smaller, rounded rocks formed a pathway in the current, and we were able to hop across to reach the middle. We talked and watched our empty litchi shells float downstream. When the sun started to set, we felt the chill in the air, and the fading light finally shook us out of our reverie. We stood up and got our balance before hopping back across the stones and collecting our things to go home.

I'll never forget that day on the mountain, the day when the sights and feelings were so foreign it was like someone else's life momentarily juxtaposed mine—the day I tried to outrun my pain.

I remember how we turned towards the mountain, coasting freely over the crisscross of yellowed roads with golden rice waving in the sun almost as far as the eye could see. The image of that glaring sun, blue sky, the golden rice, the green and brown mountains ahead, and me, flying, flying across it all…I think this scene will flood my vision with its brilliant colors in my last days.

He reached down from on high and took hold of me; he drew me out of deep waters. He rescued me from my powerful enemy, from my foes, who were too strong for me. They confronted me in the day of my disaster, but the Lord was my support. He brought me out into a spacious place; he rescued me because he delighted in me. Psalm 18

7

MY THIRD CALL

For me, Paris was not "the city of lights." It wasn't even "the city of love," despite my going there for that reason. No, Paris was for reuniting with Olivier in the hope that our relationship would finally flourish. I couldn't get out of Taiwan fast enough in my desperation to throw myself into his arms and let him rescue me from the pit I had been living in. Paris could just as easily have been Wichita, Kansas. It could have been Mongolia for all I cared.

It was early September in 1994 when I left Taiwan for good, and I planned a quick visit to the States in between moving countries. I had just ten days to put off my Asian self and don my Parisian self, never mind taking the time to find my authentic self. I was still unbalanced, and on my girls' night out to see *Forest Gump,* I spent a good portion of it hyperventilating in the bathroom stall, in quiet, heaving sobs as I tried to steady my emotions. I didn't know why I was so sad when I had someplace to go.

Finally, the long-awaited day arrived, and I paced the airport terminal in JFK, dressed in my carefully chosen baggy jeans and cranberry-colored shirt, my hair freshly permed in long, wavy curls. In Paris, I fell laughing into Olivier's arms, and suddenly the world felt right again. We headed for Angers and there received a formal welcome from his parents. I was the first girl Olivier had ever brought home, and I suppose it was quite a jump for them to skip the intermediate step of a casual, after-school girlfriend to one that would be living with them every weekend. He would do his military service in La Rochelle during the week while I stayed in Paris for my studies, and we would reunite at his parents' house on the weekends.

His family owned a beautiful, old townhouse with a dark wooden staircase leading to the second floor that held the office and parental suite and then continued up to more bedrooms on the third floor.

Our meals were always formal with a pretty cotton tablecloth and matching cloth napkins, each napkin distinguished by individual rings. I helped where I could, cutting the garlic in slivers for the salad dressing, setting out the bottle of wine and filling the water carafe, scraping the bread crumbs from the tablecloth with a little bronze dustpan. But I was hesitant to intrude. The kitchen was his mother's domain. When she set out to cook in her elegant skirt and heels, her hands busy and her mind preoccupied, there was no room for me. I never felt fully at ease at Olivier's house, but I was always grateful to be there. It was a somewhat indifferent sanctuary, but one I clung to desperately.

Soon after arriving in France, I took the train back to Paris from Angers. I was anxious to find my footing, and I needed to get an au pair position and a place to live. I'd heard that people posted their ads at the American Church, so I went there to study the possibilities.

Sure enough, the large corkboard under the awning of the church was covered with little, white index cards, differentiated at first glance only by the penmanship. There were two ads that struck me as interesting: one was for a family that had a large *chambre de bonne*—the servant's room located on the top floor of a Parisian building. This particular room included the luxury of a built-in bathroom and kitchenette. The other family lived in a nicer area and had five children.

Both positions carried benefits. A family with five kids was not going to expect me to wait on them whereas a family with one or two would likely expect just that. But then, I knew the other family's accommodations were a rarity.

I arranged to meet the large family first at their luxury Haussmannien building in the 16th *arrondissement*. I rang the doorbell and an elegant woman opened the door, whose thick blonde hair was tied back with a black ribbon. Her name was Véronique.

"Would you like some coffee?" she asked me in fluent English with a warm smile. It was pouring rain outside.

"Yes, thank you." I smiled back. The living room was cozy, a welcome contrast to the bleakness of the outdoors. As we talked, her oldest daughter came in—she looked just like her mother.

In the short forty-five-minute visit, which was more of a reprieve than an interview, I shared about the other position for which I would be interviewing. She regretfully told me she couldn't compete with the housing aspect, but I assured her I would still consider her offer and let her know after the weekend. The second employer's demeanor stood in stark contrast to the first. She was proud and rigid, and her bearing seemed to say, "You will never be part of us—you will only work for us." In the end, I chose not to.

I loved my new family, who made me feel included and treated me with affection. When the mother rebuked her children to sit upright at the table, I jumped upright with the rest of them, which made her laugh. She said I was just like one of her own daughters, except I was more obedient. With them, I absorbed the French culture and learned how to run a household—like how to fold underwear, iron linens properly, or cook traditional French meals. I soaked it all in—the family life, the rich culture, the classical language. It seemed to me if I could just grasp these things and incorporate them into who I was I would finally be worth something.

I went to the Sorbonne in the mornings, and in the afternoons, I picked the younger children up from school. In the schoolyard, I watched the children pour out of the double doors, clothed in their navy blue shorts or skirts, dark knee socks, and white button-down shirts.

When I saw this flurry of happiness, the children running up to their beaming mothers, waving a drawing they had done, I felt an intense longing to have this life for myself. I wanted my own French children who would rush up to me, to whom I would be more than just the au pair. I wanted to belong to this country. But when I looked around at the French mothers who seemed so put-together, living such vibrant lives, I knew I couldn't compete.

The children and I walked home together, crossing the large avenue overlooking the Arc de Triomphe. Their snack was usually an apple and a chunk of baguette with a strip of chocolate squares pushed through the soft interior. They ate this while walking, and they talked over each other, their mouths full of bits of apple. One spotted the new Renault Twingo car and rushed to punch his brother, crying out, "Twingo *bleu*." or "Twingo *rouge*.".

At home, I helped them with their homework, made the dinner, and drew their baths before reading them bedtime stories in my faltering French. After my duties were done, and I said goodnight to the family, I went out the back door of the kitchen into the dark, rustic staircase with peeling paint and worn wooden steps, and climbed the additional flights to my room. The cheerful, fuchsia rug and bright overhead light greeted me when I opened the door, and I walked over to the tall windows that overlooked the Parisian rooftops.

My depression crept into this seemingly idyllic life. Too often, when I was not required to be somewhere, I lay in my bed and stared at the ceiling. It might have been daytime with the sun shining, and I was in Paris, but I could only get up to take care of the children. I could only get up for duty, not for myself.

I remember lying there and wanting to die. After what happened to my brother, I didn't want to take my own life, but I had no will to live it either. I imagined floating up to the heavens, floating far away from my body and letting go of the life cord. It seemed like such a peaceful way to end my life. Week after week, these thoughts murmured in my heart as I lay alone in my room.

Sometime that fall, I went to the doctor for a sore throat. He observed me acutely for a moment in his cluttered office then started asking questions that had more to do with me than my throat. I spoke numbly about car accidents and suicides and travel and feelings of rootlessness. Finally he said, "I'm giving you a prescription for antidepressants."

I stared at him open-mouthed. I had no idea I was depressed. I mean, medicine was one step away from mental institutions—surely not something for me. "Wh...what?" I stammered. "But isn't that rather drastic?"

"No, it's actually more common than you think," he answered. "And given the past you've had with your brother and your head trauma, I think you need it."

I walked out of there with a prescription, feeling ashamed. My already low self-esteem plummeted as I thought about what people would say if they knew. I confessed my diagnosis haltingly to Olivier, who didn't quite know how to take it. I also set up an appointment to meet with the minister of the American Church because I didn't know whom else to talk to.

I sat in the church library, grateful for the pastor's time, as I told him how tired and lost I felt. I was barely able to voice the words, "I have been put on antidepressants" through the deep shame that engulfed me. He looked at me with a kindly gleam in his eye, and without saying a word, gave a mock gesture of whipping himself over his shoulder.

I laughed a little in spite of my gloomy embarrassment. "You mean it's not so bad?" I thought if a man of God didn't think antidepressants were something to be ashamed of, maybe it really wasn't so terrible to take them.

"You have to do what you need to for your health," he said. "God expects you to use all the tools you're given, and modern medicine is just one of those tools." I was relieved when I left his office but still embarrassed enough to completely ignore my doctor the one time I ran into him on the metro.

Depression is like being in a round, windowless room with a low ceiling and lots of doors. The ceiling is so low it sits on your forehead and pushes your brow down, blocking out any help from above. The doors represent solutions to your problems, but all of them are locked and you cannot exit. You cannot get out, no matter what means you try.

Within two days of being on medication, the low ceiling exploded upwards. It was gone. I didn't see a ceiling—I saw the sun. I saw the sky, far away with all its possibilities. The doors all opened. I could choose which door made the most sense for me and exit to find the correct path.

I had my reason back, and I started to sleep deeply and well. I could breathe in and smell the fresh air or the cigarette smoke floating from the cafés, mingled with the bitter aroma of espresso. There was warmth in my stomach, and I started to feel hunger. I could taste the fruity-sour wine, the piquant mustard on crispy lettuce, the warm, rich gravy in the stew.

I started to laugh again. I couldn't remember the last time I had laughed with any real joy.

Fueled by this new awareness of my senses, I chose to walk home from school rather than take the metro. I walked from the Sorbonne to the Notre Dame. I crossed over the Pont Neuf and walked along the Seine to the Louvre. From there I hiked up the Champs-Elysées and followed the curve of the Arc de Triomphe until I got to Avenue Kléber. That took me to Trocadéro with its great lawn and view of the Eiffel Tower, the splendor of France. From there, I finally arrived at my apartment, barely out of breath from a walk that took just under two hours. In that way, Paris became mine.

Every Friday, I took the TGV to Angers to stay with Olivier's family. We spent our weekends going for bike rides along the Loire, the fall foliage creating shady paths along the river. We saw a movie and wandered around town, peering into the shops that lined the cobblestone streets for pedestrians. I examined the window display of the Geneviève Lethu shop for French household goods, wondering what it would be like to have a wedding registry there, hungry for such a thing to happen to me too. Were it not for the time ticking away and the uncertainty of our future, I might have been happy contemplating these things.

I was excited to spend Christmas with his family, to be with him and a part of everything for an entire week. We ate all the usual elegant holiday foods—goose stuffed with chestnuts, smoked salmon, champagne—and I lovingly wrapped my gifts for each family member, hoping they would be pleased. I watched their smiles as they opened the CDs and scarves—as Olivier opened his sweater, the leather gloves, and the book he had wanted to read.

Olivier gave me a small pocket atomizer to spray cologne. That was it. There was no new perfume to show he thought of me as something worth spending money on, or that he even cared what scent I was wearing. My face was so hot I couldn't look up from the gift. It was impossible to hide my disappointment from him or his family—dismay over the fact that our relationship seemed as empty in his eyes as that stupid atomizer. Christmas in France lost its magic that year.

On New Year's Eve, I accompanied him to a military ball where he introduced me to the general as his fiancée. Fiancée. My heart leapt at the word and I held my breath, waiting to see if he had something to ask me. But he didn't say anything at all. As the night wore on, I finally questioned him about it, and he explained that he had only used the word to seem stable and serious.

That night, the general, whom Olivier thought so highly of, asked me to dance the waltz. The room spun by in a blur as I whirled around in his arms, my boyfriend watching us from the table with an unreadable expression. When the evening was over, we walked back to my room in silence. We walked and walked late at night, too tired to speak, in the empty streets of Paris because we couldn't get a taxi.

The year passed by in this somewhat disconsolate way with a few bright memories that seemed to let me know God was present in the darkness. One late night, I was heading up to my seventh floor studio. I rarely ever saw anyone in those other apartments, but on this particular night, the couple next to me happened to be climbing up to their studio right behind me. We exchanged hellos and entered our respective rooms.

As soon as I opened my door, I knew something was wrong. The window, which I had left cracked earlier, was now wide open, and the curtains were blowing in the breeze. I heard movement, a scratching sound coming from near the window. Terrified, I gathered my courage and crept closer to the corner, peering in between the armoire and the wall.

Two beady eyes stared back at me before the scratching began again with renewed vigor. I jumped back, and then—I didn't know what to do. I couldn't sleep there with that creature, so I had to find a solution. I knocked on my neighbor's door. At least I knew they were there and still awake. Perhaps they could tell me what to do. I explained the situation in between apologies.

As it turned out, the young man was the son of a veterinarian and wasn't in the least afraid of animals. He went to have a look, figured out that a crow had gotten stuck behind the armoire and didn't know how to get out on its own. He wrapped his arm with a tee shirt and let the bird latch on. He then opened the window wider and brought his arm to the sill. After a moment's hesitation, the crow took off. I watched the bird soar into the night air, my terror taking flight with it.

What I was feeling in that moment went beyond simple gratitude to my neighbor—it stretched its tendrils to the heavens in something resembling faith. How could I not remark that the only time I ever saw any of my neighbors in the entire year was just at a time, late at night, when I was alone and desperately needed help. And he was just the one who was able to give it. It seemed like more than coincidence.

I had begun to read the Bible in my quiet moments, ever since it had been given to me in Taiwan. I also met with another Christian counselor. We spoke more about God than my troubles—at my request—and I was watching my faith grow with some degree of surprise. One time she told me that I could pray Jesus into my heart to be saved. "Don't ever let anyone tell you that you need to do anything other than pray Jesus into your heart to be saved," she said emphatically.

I had heard this before and didn't have any particular feeling or conviction attached to it. But I thought I should perhaps give it a go. I was walking down the street as I decided to do this. I felt kind of funny but said to myself, "Okay. If this is what I'm supposed to do, I guess I'll try it."

So I took a deep breath and said inwardly, Um. Jesus?" I kept walking. "I open the door to my heart so you can come in.

Suddenly I felt a little sick and I stopped walking. No, I felt more than sick. I felt invaded and started wringing my hands away from my body, retracting quickly. *No, no—get out. Get out. I don't know you.*

I may not have been ready for any kind of commitment, but I was searching for *something*. I went to the midweek Bible studies that were held at the American Cathedral. I remember once that the subject of pre-marital sex came up in these studies, and I said to the minister,

"But...that doesn't actually apply in today's world." He replied gently, "Well—it's supposed to." I was surprised to hear it but was inspired to try the celibacy route for a few nights while sleeping in my boyfriend's bed...

I discovered during this time that I wasn't able to live the life of a religious person, but I persevered in some kind of religious pursuit because I just loved the Bible. I began to wonder...Did God actually love me? I mean, did He even notice me? Of all the billions of people wandering around the earth?

One day I was musing about this as I stood at my window, staring out at the cloudy sky and gray tiles of the Parisian rooftops. My heart budded with a small hope, and I spoke to God directly for the first time in my adulthood.

"Do you even know I'm here? Do you love me?"

A huge ray of sun broke through the gray clouds. I could see it piercing a hole in the sky as it came to settle directly on my face. I was so astonished, my face lit up with joy. "Thank you. Thank you," I whispered.

As quickly as it had come, the light was swallowed up by the gray clouds again.

A couple months before I left Paris, I was strolling down Avenue George V—exploring, dreaming of becoming a French wife and mother, examining the shops as was my custom. A woman stopped me on the street and asked, "Do you speak English?"

"Yes, I'm American," I replied.

"Well," she began with a warm smile, "I just wanted to know if you would like to come to my church. It's really great—lots of young people and English speakers too. We have Bible studies..." she trailed away as she looked at me expectantly. I could hear in her accent that she was American too.

Still, I shook my head regretfully. There was no way I was ever going to go to a church where a stranger had invited me. I mistrusted what they would teach me and was afraid of becoming a religious person, blindly following the indoctrinated masses. That whole scenario was beyond contemplation.

Yet somehow, I was touched in spite of it all that she had reached out to me, and in the past year, my heart had softened towards all things pertaining to God. So I smiled at her to cushion my rejection and said, "Keep up the good work though."

I was encouraging someone to share her faith. Something had shifted in my heart, and it seemed like a major fault line was forming between who I had been and who I was becoming.

As the tectonic plates of my soul shifted, God remained unmoved. That was His third call.

No, in all these things we are more than conquerors through him who loved us. For I am convinced that neither death nor life, neither angels nor demons, neither the present nor the future, nor any powers, neither height nor depth, nor anything else in all creation, will be able to separate us from the love of God that is in Christ Jesus our Lord. Romans 8

8

THE TIME I ANSWERED

I extended my stay in Paris by a month to help the family pack for a two-year move to Dijon. I was hoping that Olivier would realize he didn't want me to leave, the more imminent my departure became. When he didn't show any signs of anguish, I pushed it back yet again.

In spite of it all, I was quietly content that month, spending all day carefully organizing and packing their entire apartment in calm solitude. The summer light flooded through the tall French windows, and I sat on the herringbone wooden floors, carefully sorting the colorful pieces to children's games and wrapping the china plates in newspaper. I found order in the perfectly wrapped boxes, which I couldn't find in my own life. When the final day arrived, Olivier and I spent our last evening in my little empty room with my suitcases shoved against the wall.

I got a horrible bladder infection that night. It went from uncomfortable to bleeding, pain shooting up my spinal cord, in just a few short hours. I was terrified, knowing I wouldn't be able to travel in that state but not knowing what to do. Olivier was no help, which made me feel lonelier than ever. That night, I tossed and turned in pain and anxiety next to a distant boyfriend who was fast asleep.

We planned to leave for the airport at noon the following day, and

Olivier went to the FNAC store to look at CDs. I couldn't go anywhere in my state, and with my frequent trips to the toilet, but it occurred to me that the pharmacy on the corner might be able to help. As soon as I stepped into the bright sunlit morning, I bumped into the concierge of the building. She saw my troubled face and immediately asked me what was wrong.

"I have a bladder infection," I said, feeling both ashamed and gripped by worry. "And I have to leave for the airport in two hours."

"Oh." Her face showed concern. "Well I happen to be going to the doctor right now to bring my son, and you don't need an appointment. Why don't you come with me?"

I was able to see the doctor quickly, he gave me a prescription for antibiotics that I was able to fill immediately, and the medicine took effect within the hour. So the only pain I felt upon leaving Paris was from the promptness in which Olivier rushed me through Departures. I stepped on the escalator going up through the Plexiglas tubes of Charles de Gaulle, and he was gone before I was halfway up.

My father quickly saw that it would be impossible for me to live at home and get a job in the small city where I had grown up. Too much had happened, I had seen so much, I was so changed...But I had spent all my savings in Paris and didn't know where else to go. Goaded by two weeks of my testy speech and despairing attitude, he finally came into my room one day.

"Jennie, I'm loaning you two thousand dollars to move to New York so you can get a job there," he said somewhat sternly. "I want you to pay it back, but not in piecemeal—I want you to pay the entire lump sum in two year's time."

I was so relieved I immediately rushed into his arms. Whether he fully understood all the emotions that were causing me to slowly drown, I couldn't say; but he understood enough to throw me a lifeline.

My father softened. "Well, we can both see that it's not going to work with you living here," he said, patting my back.

With this hopeful prospect before me, I suddenly came to life again. My father gave me the check on a Tuesday, and I immediately answered a few advertisements for jobs, setting up interviews for that

Thursday. I threw my luggage and myself on the first train I could get to Manhattan, this time determined to find an office job with steady pay. I had decided I was finally ready to settle down.

Once again, my college friend Gideon welcomed me into her home, though she was married by now, pregnant, and living in New Jersey. I stayed with them for a few days until I could get my bearings. I was also invited to stay with two high school friends in the area, so I could pop from one place to another without outwearing my welcome.

I was desperate. I knew that two thousand dollars would not go far in Manhattan. By that stage in my life, I had nothing left but what I was about to build. I didn't have a home to return to—I had only borrowed money, no career, no living situation, and no one to rely on. I had *one* ambition, and that was to get an apartment and a job with health insurance as soon as was earthly possible. My first night at Gideon's house, I threw myself down on my knees with the bedroom door closed and begged God to bless me.

I was interviewing everywhere I could. I had a notebook full of cards from the agencies I met with, and since the job market was favorable, there were many job opportunities. The position I most wanted was with an international financial newspaper. The staff was young and vibrant, and though I knew next to nothing about finance or journalism, I was attracted to the lively, international atmosphere in the office. The company called me for three back-to-back interviews, and I was anxious because I knew I would have to accept the first offer I got, even if it meant working for another company.

Finally, I was sitting on the edge of my chair in front of the chief financial officer's desk and eagerly answering his inquiries. "Yes. I can work long hours," and "Yes. $23,000 starting salary is acceptable." Then I heard the magical words, "We'd like to offer you the position," which made me clap my hands and squeal with delight. The CFO and manager smiled at my eagerness.

This crowning success occurred at the same time that Gideon connected me to someone looking for a roommate for her huge Upper West Side apartment. *How was it possible?* I wondered. I got the job of my dreams and the apartment of my dreams in exactly one week upon arriving in New York City. It seemed that "as soon as earthly possible" had nothing on "as soon as heavenly possible" as God magically brought all the pieces together.

For my new position, I assisted the sales team in selling advertising space and setting up conferences for the IMF/World Bank and regional development bank meetings. All around the office, I heard the journalists and editors yelling at each other over deadlines, and the sales staff speaking Spanish, Portuguese, Japanese, and Russian as they made connections with bankers and financial gurus all around the world. I nervously—and proudly—added my French and Mandarin to the woven medley of languages.

My new roommate was a trial sketch artist. She lived in a pre-war apartment overlooking the Hudson River, and I had my own room and bathroom. The sunken living room boasted large windows and high ceilings and was painted in white. My bedroom was furnished with a large comfortable bed, a dresser, and a spacious desk. The bathroom, although old, had a glass shower with strong jet showerheads on the tiled walls and ceiling. It was the first time in my adult life that my living space was a haven and not just someplace to sleep.

My roommate was depressed at the time. She was older than I was by about twenty years and had lost the love of her life in a car accident the year prior. At that time, I could relate to this deep depression of hers but had come out of mine, so we were able to be what we needed for each other.

I never saw her eat anything but tahini straight out of the can. She was so depressed she couldn't eat, and out of desperation, chose the most calorie dense food she could find just to survive. I cleaned and organized her kitchen and started cooking her food to encourage her to eat. We connected in those rare times she was home and not staying at her new boyfriend's apartment (whom she didn't love—he didn't make her laugh in the same way).

Every morning I took the 1/9 train down to SoHo, exalting in the feeling of being cultured—even sophisticated—in my new life. I was still dressing with a French flair, with navy cardigans and silk scarves around my neck, but I was starting to add elements of black to my wardrobe, inspired by the New York scene. I bought a bagel and coffee at the deli next to our office before climbing the stairs and throwing myself into anything that needed to be done. With all the conferences and meetings, there was no shortage of work, yet my colleagues and I still found time to have leisurely lunches, working late hours to catch up. We had all the freedom of the young and unattached. I was happy.

Shortly after I started working, I was sitting on the crowded train at morning rush hour when a young woman nearly toppled onto me as the train swerved. She made a joke about the cramped quarters, and I looked up in good humor, happy to see someone break out of the Manhattan mold and talk to me. She was only on the train for one stop, but she offered to exchange numbers, so I did. Her name was Genieve.

It seems odd to have done that in retrospect, but she was friendly and I had so few friends. There was also something about her that I immediately trusted. Years later, our friendship still strong, we would stand in each other's weddings so my trust had been well placed. After quickly scribbling down our numbers, she stepped off the train, and I found myself alone, blushing, as people stared at me curiously.

A few days later I was at work, and the internal storm of activity rushed to a standstill, replaced by a sort of emptiness. I had been so busy moving, working, and living my new life I'd barely had time to think. But in an instant, my whirling mind was on pause. I stopped typing, held captive by a thought, and I stared at the screen without really seeing it. I started praying silently at my desk.

"God, you gave me everything I asked for—a job, an apartment, and they are so perfect for me. Now I need to find a church, so I can find you. I pray that you will lead me someplace where people love the Bible as much as I do. Oh, and maybe lots of young people so I can relate—"

The phone rang, interrupting my silent prayer. When I picked the receiver up, it was Genieve. We chatted for a few minutes, and I told her where I worked. We discovered that we both lived on the Upper West Side.

At my mention of 104th Street, she said, "Oh, there's this cute little café right on the corner of your street where I go all the time to read my Bible."

It struck me forcibly that she would talk about the Bible when I had just been in the middle of praying, and I couldn't hold back from squeaking out a high-pitched, "Oh." But there was no way I was going to talk about anything Bible-related at work, so I glossed over it and we made plans to meet for coffee a few days later.

I didn't want to wait to find a church, so the next morning, I called her and left a message saying I was interested in coming to her church. I qualified my message with a list of unacceptable churches, so I could back out in case she was into something weird. After leaving the message, I went out to get a haircut.

I was sitting in the hairdresser's chair, watching the woman in the mirror behind me as she examined the picture I brought showing the style I wanted. She said, "This photo looks just like a girl who's always inviting me to her church."

I murmured politely. All this Bible and church talk that kept cropping up with strangers seemed both odd and natural at the same time. She continued, "Yeah, she goes to this church with a lot of performers and singers, and they meet at the Fashion High School."

I scrunched up my nose and said, "What? Performers meeting in a high school? What kind of church can that be?" She responded with a shrug. "Well, you never know where you'll find God."

How true.

After I got home, Genieve called me back. Chuckling at my "list," she explained that her church was none of the ones I wanted to avoid. It was just a regular church that followed the Bible. And they met at the Fashion High School.

We agreed to meet on the front steps the next morning, but when I arrived for the service, I looked into the auditorium, and there was almost no one there. There were a few people setting up sound equipment and a few more talking in the aisles, but it didn't have the lively ambiance I expected. I turned around and thought to myself, *this feels strange. It doesn't feel like a church...and where is everybody?* I started to consider the pretty stone church I had seen on Broadway and Tenth Street.

As I turned to go, I was stopped by a voice. "So you're here an hour early too, huh?"

"What?" I asked, turning back around.

"It's Daylight Savings time and we got here early. The service doesn't start for another hour."

Ah. Okay, so that explained things. This young man was from French-speaking Africa, so when he asked me if I wanted to have coffee while waiting for the service to start, I agreed. I longed to connect to the world of French speakers I had just left. The hour passed quickly as we talked at a nearby diner. When it was time for the service to begin, we each went our separate ways. Genieve waved me over and introduced me to her friends.

Many things about that service impressed me. There were a lot of young people, and the friends Genieve introduced me to couldn't have formed a more diverse band.

She herself had grown up on the Upper East Side, one of the few black women to attend her private school. She went on to study Philosophy, Dance, and French at Yale. (Many years later, she married and moved to Boston where she got her master's at the rival school, Harvard.) Dishell came from more modest roots in Harlem. She spoke with serenity and strength about growing up on welfare with her mother in and out of prison. Then there was Grace. She was Taiwanese, of all things, living in New York and working in fashion. I surprised her with my rusty Mandarin, and we connected instantly, talking about her country.

I absolutely loved the whole lot of them. That was my idea of friendship—a group of people who don't resemble each other at all in race, education, or social standing, but whose hearts connect. That was the kind of church to which I wanted to belong.

Then there was the singing. Loud, energetic, glorious, and perfectly in tune—important to a classical girl like me. The preacher was dynamic, and his message was funny and real, cutting straight to my heart. Everything he said was so honest and raw, I was wiping away tears the entire time from laughter and…I'm not even sure what else in the myriad emotions I felt.

Nevertheless, I clammed back up after the service, afraid to show the depth of my feelings. "How did you like it?" Genieve asked when it was over.

I shrugged my shoulders and said, "It was alright." I was too proud to say that it was just what I needed, that I loved it, that it had moved me, and that I was hungry for more. She invited me to lunch, and after we had finished eating, asked me if I was interested in studying the Bible.

"Um," I hedged. "I'd be open to sharing Scriptures together, but I don't want you to teach me anything," blithely unaware of the pride it took to say something like that.

She graciously agreed, yet when we opened the Bible, it was clear that for all my extensive reading over the past year and a half, I didn't understand it nearly as well as she did. As we spoke, my conscience started bothering me about the things I knew I should be putting into practice. Longing to be honest but feeling uncomfortable at the same time, I said to her, "I think I do follow all of this…except for one area."

"Your boyfriend?" she ventured.

"Yes." I had gained awareness from the pastor in France that there was some sort of expectation of purity involved in following God. I mean—I knew there was this expectation if I was going to do this thing seriously. But I was also testing her. She was my age; surely she would understand the struggle involved and "let me off the hook," so to speak.

But she just nodded and said, "Yeah." There was no judgment in her expression in spite of the fact that her one word implied a challenge. I respected her for telling me the truth and appreciated that it came without judgment. It made me more willing to hear what she had to say.

My boyfriend and I…were we even a couple anymore? When were we going to see each other again? Did he take the relationship as seriously as I did? The last time we had spoken on the phone, he talked about his job and how he planned to go to Spain for his next vacation. I was floored. If he could think about going anywhere else than to see me, this relationship must really have no future. But that was so hard to see after three years of being together. I really couldn't believe it had come to this.

I was troubled and decided to write a letter breaking up with him. True, I didn't want to be with someone who didn't want to be with me, but I also hoped that he would be so horrified at the thought of losing me he would propose marriage. So I sent the letter off, telling him when he could reach me to discuss it.

I expected his call a week and a half later on a Sunday morning and told Genieve I wouldn't be going to church with her because of it. I waited for the call, beside myself with anxiety, and when the phone rang, I picked it up with trembling fingers. His starting words were encouraging; he had cried all afternoon when he read my letter. Then the floor fell out from under me as he continued. "But then I realized you were right. This relationship has no future and it's not fair to you. I think you're right to end it."

Oh...oh...I never thought he would call my bluff. I asked him, "Do you want to break up with me?"

"No," he replied.

"Don't...don't you want to marry me?"

But apparently—no. We spoke for a half-hour, and I tried everything I could think of to get him to see reason, but he had made up his mind. So we ended the relationship with that call, and I collapsed on the floor in tears.

Genieve checked in with me after church. I sobbed out the details of the conversation, and she immediately said she was coming over. An hour later she was at my door with lunch, a listening ear, and hugs. How much I needed that—someone who was willing to break through convention for a new friend. It didn't matter to her that she barely knew me; she saw my need and was there.

I took Monday off to mourn, and the next day I went back to work. Honestly, I don't know how I was able to get over the break-up so quickly and resist any urge to call or write him. It probably helped that we were in different countries, and I had an exciting life to jump into. I threw myself into my job and even agreed to study the Bible a few more times, grateful for the friends I had made at both work and church.

We were doing theme studies, which gave an order to the Bible I had not yet grasped. I learned what it took to be a disciple, why Jesus died on the Cross, what it meant to be baptized—basic Christian building blocks. But I was still not comfortable being in the learner's seat.

Once when I was at Genieve's house studying with her and Grace about the crucifixion, I finally turned to her in annoyance and said, "Why are you asking *me* all the questions? What about her?" lurching my head towards Grace.

Genieve answered gently. "Grace has already done all these studies. So I have I." Then looking at me pointedly, she added, "Why don't you want to learn?"

Aargh! That was the right thing to say to me because I *did* want to learn. I had an insatiable thirst to learn everything I could, and when it came to the Bible, how much more did I crave understanding? I didn't put up any more open fuss, but my answers were still clipped and proud. I didn't want to let anyone see too deeply into my heart. I didn't want to be vulnerable.

On my twenty-fifth birthday, a few weeks after coming to church for the first time, I woke up sick. I had never felt like that before. My chest was so heavy I could barely draw a breath. I was so weak I had to crawl to the bathroom. I knew there was no way I could make it to work, so I crawled over to the phone to call in sick. I didn't even have the strength to walk those few steps to the desk. I called my boss on the phone, crying—I was so sick and it was my birthday. I lay in bed all day, miserable and alone.

That night, Genieve, Dishell, and Grace came over with balloons and cards. In my pitiable state I had called Genieve to tell her I was sick, so they also brought hot soup and sat around me while I sipped it. I wanted to cry from relief at being so cared for. I couldn't remember the last time I had felt like that.

By the time I was well enough to study the Bible again, all my defenses were down. I could see that what they were teaching me in the Bible was true. I recognized that what they taught held a sort of fundamental truth, which applied to me.

I could also see that their love for me was genuine and their standard for applying the Bible in their own lives consistent, so I started to trust them. I jumped into the studies with an enthusiasm I had not shown before and started to express my desire to make a commitment to God, to be baptized, and to leave my old way of life behind.

However, I didn't fully realize what that meant. When I announced

I was ready to get baptized, we did a final study to make sure I was ready. The night we got together, we touched back on the subject of my old boyfriend. When they asked me where I would stay if I went back to Paris, I replied that I would sleep on his couch. Naturally.

Rebecca, who had joined the studies more recently, and whose strength of character and faith I admired, simply asked, "Well, what kind of temptation could that sleeping arrangement lead to?"

My jaw dropped, and I became hot with anger as I understood the implications of what she was saying. "You mean to tell me I can only marry someone in this church?"

But what I meant was, "You mean I won't be able to do whatever I want anymore?"

I finally understood I was not making a decision that I could later toss away when it was inconvenient. That's not who I was anyway. The cost of changing my life would be giving up my dream of being married to this French man—a dream I shockingly still held on to—and that I would turn aside from that dream in favor of marrying someone who had the same faith and convictions I had. At the time, I couldn't see how important that was; I could only see the cost of what I had to give up.

I was heartbroken, and slowly said, "I'm sorry. I can't do it. I can't get baptized. I'm not ready for this kind of commitment."

There were no reproaches—after all, it was my decision. We started gathering our belongings to go home, and I was feeling sorry for myself. Genieve grabbed my arm and said briskly, "Come on. Let's go get some Chinese food."

I looked at her in surprise. *Are you kidding me? I'm just making the most important decision of my life—to turn away from God—and you want to go eat?*

But she insisted, and I had nowhere else to go. I'm sure she sensed I would benefit from some company in my current emotional state. As we ate, we hardly touched on the emotionally wrenching talk we had just had and instead spoke about movies.

At the end of the meal, I reached down and grabbed one of the fortune cookies sitting on the dark red plate and opened it mechanically. But when I read it, my eyes grew wide and my mouth flew open.

Genieve looked up at me, saw my face and giggled. "Okay—what? What does it say?"

I handed the slip of paper to her, and she read it out loud. "Your secret desire to completely change your life will manifest itself."

We looked at each other and both started laughing. "Yeah, I don't think God is done with you yet," she said.

The next day I woke up determined to become a Christian. The night's sleep had shaken off any doubts. I have no idea how this complete about-face happened. Although, if I am honest, it might possibly have had something to do with the fact that there was no shortage of handsome men in the church, and I had come to realize how foolish it was to hold out for one who didn't even want me. That night we all met at Sissi's apartment, a few blocks over, and I got baptized in her bathtub, surrounded by friends.

As I started getting accustomed to the new church culture I was part of, I pieced everything together and realized that the person who had invited me to church in Honolulu, the person who had invited me in New York, the person who had invited me in Paris, and then Genieve who invited me in New York again all went to the same church. They were sister churches in different cities, but the same church nonetheless.

In fact, the person who invited me in Paris, Marie, eventually moved back to her hometown of New York and ended up becoming Genieve's roommate. When I first met her, she seemed familiar, but I couldn't figure out why. It finally dawned on me that I had met her before, and I couldn't wait to see her again to confirm my suspicions. I bounded up to her. "Marie, you used to go to the church in Paris, right?"

"Yes," she said.

"Did you ever invite people on the street to go to church?"

"All the time," she said. "Why?"

"Do you remember meeting me? On Avenue George V? It was morning, and I told you to keep up the good work?" I asked smiling.

"Oh my gosh. That was you? You had long hair then," she remembered with surprise. And then as an afterthought, "Why didn't you come to church when I asked you?"

"I don't know," I said, laughing with delight. "I guess I just wasn't ready."

God had extended His hand once again, and by this time, the darkness that threatened to engulf me had finally dissipated so I was able to see my way. I lowered my battle-weary fists and sat cross-legged at the feet of the one who had been coaxing me for as long as I could remember. The one whose presence was so near and consistent it could be felt.

Genieve was my fourth call from God. And this time, I answered Him.

And have you completely forgotten this word of encouragement that addresses you as a father addresses his son? It says, 'My son, do not make light of the Lord's discipline, and do not lose heart when he rebukes you, because the Lord disciplines the one he loves, and he chastens everyone he accepts as his son.' Endure hardship as discipline; God is treating you as his children. No discipline seems pleasant at the time, but painful. Later on, however, it produces a harvest of righteousness and peace for those who have been trained by it. Hebrews 12

9

SOBER

I thought becoming a Christian meant that my life would finally spin neatly into place, my problems relegated to a distant memory. As if to prove this fact, I even managed successfully to go off anti-depressants. *The Spirit is my new happy pill,* I thought.

I hadn't bargained for some of the hurdles—learning to be unembarrassed about my new life as a Christian; surrendering to unmet expectations and disappointments in a church full of human frailty; coming to terms with my own weaknesses and believing I was still worth something; and last, but not least, abandoning my autonomy in favor of obedience to God. That lesson was the hardest.

Oblivious to these obstacles at first, I was naively happy. It wasn't so much in being "saved" that I found my joy. I was happier about belonging to a church full of young, dynamic people, half of which were men. I was happy that I had finally found the path to perfection, although I was not self aware enough to admit it. Everything was new and shiny. I had been married to Christ and was on my honeymoon with his church. Oh, but how brief the honeymoon was before the divine discipline began.

It was almost inevitable that I would be unprepared. How could I not be seduced when my once-lonely life became a whirlwind of activity, friendship, and this new element of fellowship—the shared faith that drew the diverse lot of us together. All of this was happening in the exciting city of New York, which suddenly grew intimate in the face of such extended family.

I had, as yet, only added to the pleasure of my life and had given little up in return. I lived in my luxury Upper West Side apartment, but I was almost never home. I went to the office and basked in the lively international atmosphere, often staying late to work overtime and eat dinner with my colleagues. I went out with Christian friends in the evenings to church events or simply for a night on the town. The few evenings I was home early were treasured instead of lonely.

To add the exquisite to the sublime, I went out on dates. The men in the church were gentlemen. They picked me up, they brought me home, they opened doors for me, and they paid for everything. I'm sure I fell in love with somebody new every week.

It soon became apparent that in the midst of this menagerie of fulfillment, I still had one foot out the door on my new life. I wasn't loyal yet; I wasn't convinced. God had given me clear signs leading me to this particular church, but I had shunned the concept of becoming religious for so long. I was still afraid of having joined a cult. I don't know why I was so doubtful of my ability to discern right from wrong, but I didn't want to end up on the cover of *Time* magazine with bloated purple legs from having drunk the wrong Kool-Aid. Instead of joining in whole-heartedly, I continued cautiously, praying for assurance that I was in the right place.

My panacea for doubt came in the form of Marcia Hill. Marcia was visiting the church at the time, and we easily fell to talking and made plans to meet up outside of church. She was older and had a son named Jack who was about my age. "My Jack is going to be the President of the United States one day," she used to tell me, although he was in engineering, not politics. She also hinted broadly that I would make a fine president's wife and was eager to introduce us, but I wiggled out of committing to anything.

The more time we spent together, the more I found something "off" about her. She gave me a book of her revelations and prophecies about God, which she had written while spending a few months in a psychiatric ward. Alarmed, I began to inch away in our dealings.

One early weekday morning, the phone rang. It was Marcia, speaking in her usual Southern drawl. "Jennie," she said. "I'm going to go to Grand Central Station today to hand out my flyers, and I was praying this morning about how hard it is for me to carry the boxes and do this on my own. And then God revealed to me that you need to come with me and help."

I was horrified at the prospect. "No, I have to go to work."

She replied, "Well Jesus said to leave everything and come follow me."

I shot back, "Well you're not Jesus."

So she changed tactics, and broached the subject again of when I might be able to meet her son Jack. I cut her off. "Listen. I'm not interested in meeting your son—ever. I don't trust him because I don't trust you. I'm not comfortable with you, and I think your spiritual views are way off."

There was a sharp intake of breath before she spat out, "You ought to be spanked, spanked, spanked, spanked, spanked." Then she started speaking in tongues. I hung up, my eyes wide and my heart thumping in my chest.

A couple seconds later, she called back, and when I didn't pick up, she cooed eerily into the voicemail, "Jeeeeeenie. I know you're theeeere." Then sharply, "Pick up the phone."

There was a silence, then a soft chanting that slowly crescendoed. "Jack and Jennie went up the hill to fetch a pail of water—living water, living water, living water. I am the Hill. Marcia Hill." This inspired prophecy went on for a bit before the phone finally went dead. I fell trembling, limp, at the foot of my bed. I mean, this woman knew where I lived.

I had the inspiration to open the Bible, and it fell on the page with Isaiah 51. *I, even I, am He who comforts you. Who are you that you fear mortal men, the sons of men, who are but grass.*

Upon reading this, the peace that came over me was instantaneous. There was absolutely nothing she—a mere mortal—could do to harm me. This encounter set my own fears to rest. From then on I threw myself back into the comparative sanity of my church without a backward glance.

Once I had embraced being part of the church, I became concerned with which part of the hierarchy I would belong to—where I would fit in. Our church was organized so no one would get lost in the shuffle. Everyone was part of a Bible Talk, and everyone spent time with a "discipling partner." In addition to Sunday service, we also attended a midweek service. Everyone took part in studying the Bible with people who wanted to know more about God.

Even if one readily accepts organized religion, it's easy to see how, with such a formalized system in place, things could become rigid—stronger characters overrunning weaker ones—or taking the special care in helping a young Christian get spiritually strong and applying it across the board to mature Christians who have other needs.

Having one of the stronger characters, I tended to err on the side of legalism and mistaken superiority rather than finding myself in the position of being overrun. It was too long in my faith before I learned that love is how we treat people; it is not based on how we feel about them or how much we like and admire them. Love is an action, not a feeling.

I was quickly put in charge of leading a small Bible Talk. It seemed only natural that it should be so, and I briskly put all my energy into crushing their spirits. It was not long before God had mercy on those people, and I was taken out of leadership and removed from the privileged meetings that went along with it. This was done with kindness and respect, but I still felt the heavy weight of failure in not being publicly recognized as a spiritual leader anymore.

Instead, I was given a discipling partner who I was sure had nothing to teach me. I began to meet with her as was expected, spurning her kindness and gentle wisdom, quietly bemoaning the fact that I was doomed to fade into obscurity in the eyes of the church leadership. To add insult to injury, I was also asked to accompany someone who was going through the church program for alcoholism recovery, something I considered to be a waste of my time and talent.

The group met once a week in people's apartments, and the participants were required to come with a partner who had either completed the program, or who had never struggled with addiction. For each person, the length of the program could last anywhere from a few months to over a year, depending, honestly, on how vulnerable or smug they were.

As I sat on the living room floor next to the woman I was accompanying, I was vaguely aware of the fact that I resented being there. I wasn't sure what to expect, but I knew I had to resign myself to these Sunday afternoon meetings for some time to come. I looked up as the meeting began and Kira detailed the requirements.

I listened somewhat distractedly to what all the addicts would be required to do, looking around at the women, wondering which ones struggled with addiction and which ones were accompanying. Then I heard Kira say, "If you're here as a partner to those in recovery, you agree to abstain from all alcohol use for the duration of your participation in CR."

That got my attention. I don't know why I did this, but being incurably honest, I raised my hand and said, "I didn't know that."

Kira looked directly at me. "Is that going to be a problem for you?"

"No," I lied.

After an hour of listening to people share about their addiction, my conscience was ringing alarm bells inside my head. Too much of what people shared were things I could have shared myself. When the meeting concluded, I reluctantly went up to Kira and choked out the words, "Um. I think I need to be here for myself."

Thus began my stint in CR, somewhere between a few months and a year—somewhere between vulnerable and smug.

I had to write a journal of the first time I drank until the last time, noting how much I drank each time and what the consequences were. Then I needed to fill in every significant step in between—how often, how much, the consequences. I wrote down the requirements for the journal and then went home to work on it.

A few weeks later, it was my turn to read my journal in front of the group. I read dully, without looking up, divorced from my feelings. The words that spilled out of my mouth were embarrassing and nonsensical—there was no way these crazy ploys of youth could indicate a more serious, underlying problem. I giggled as I read, blushing as I listed the consequences of my actions and the numerous scrapes I had gotten myself into. One of the recovering addicts in the group interrupted and challenged me on the spot. "Why are you laughing? None of the rest of us thinks this is funny."

I managed to finish the remainder of the journal with a straight face, but honestly I still found the things I had done funny, the usual dereliction of youth, that it wasn't that bad. After all, I never drank during the day—except for those college parties that started early. I didn't drink every night—except for senior year in college towards the end when we were trying to soak in every last experience. I could even go to the bar and not drink a drop—sometimes.

But I did love the rebellion, the feeling of getting away with something, even from the first time I drank in high school. I was afraid of the effect, so I cautiously sipped a wine cooler until I felt the high kick in. I was thrilled that I could handle it and still be in control. I had achieved adulthood, and with it, liberty.

The next time I drank was when I spent the night at a friend's house. I arrived late and tried to catch up by drinking vodka straight. I had no idea that it would be stronger than wine coolers, or that it would hit me so fast I would find myself staggering back and forth, unable to control my movements or speech. That night I threw up in my friend's shoes and all over her carpet and passed out right before her dad came home.

And the rest of it—the dancing on tables in bars, the many, many affairs that would not have happened sober, the college nickname of "Camp" I earned from my sorority when I got wasted and hooked up with a visiting alumni who had pitched his tent in the church parking lot (where I forgot my bra the next morning)—all that was cute right?

But as I voiced these things out loud, I was covered in shame. There was shame buried so deep it didn't even make it into the journal, like the time I made a pass at a married man while staying with friends in Hawaii. Their neighbor, whose wife was away, showed friendly interest in the fact that I had learned to speak Chinese. I wasn't used to being treated so kindly and mistook his attention for something else. One night I got drunk and hit on him; he turned me away so subtly, I almost could not understand the significance of what I had done.

There were the motorcycle rides home from the bars in Taiwan, drunk without a helmet. There was the time I passed out facedown outside our college apartment, so people had to step over my inert body to get to their apartments. There was the time I staggered back into a college Christmas formal, my dress ripped up to my waist and leaves in my hair, my borrowed pearl necklace lost in the shrubbery, all because of some interlude I'd had. Then there was the time I lurched and staggered home alone at night on the wide streets of Manhattan after having gotten drunk at a company Christmas party. The next day was humiliating as I fielded off the mocking comments and sideways glances.

When I was done reading my journal, I had a complacent half-smile on my face. Never mind that I had put myself in the program. I fully expected to be exonerated, to be told that I didn't belong there after all, that mine was the foolish drinking of youth and not the real problem of an alcoholic.

Instead, Kira looked straight at me and said, "If you were not so proud, you would probably already be on the streets, homeless from your addiction." That wiped the smug look off my face.

In the months that followed, I learned how easy it was for an addict to be deceitful about his or her own heart, to hide behind layers, subterfuge, and lies. I learned to challenge the ways I deceived myself, like thinking that making a fool out of myself was cute. In spelling out the consequences publicly, I started feeling the pain of what I had done and connecting it to the substance abuse. I learned to cut through excuses and tears (my own and other people's) and get to the heart of the matter. I accepted correction without bristling, and I gave it with gentleness and respect.

In the months I spent in CR, a major change occurred in my character, perhaps more than I had ever undergone before. I was such a mix of pride and insecurity. In one breath I could think I was above someone, and in the next, that I was not worth the shoes on their feet.

But there came a day when I didn't resent going to CR every week. There came a day when I didn't care whether or not I was in leadership in the church, a day when I truly believed there was something I could learn from anyone, and that it didn't matter who discipled me. There came a day when I knew without a doubt that if I drank again, I couldn't guarantee never to fall into excess. I came to feel that my faith hinged on my sobriety. If I turned away from God and fell back into my former patterns, I'm not sure I would ever return.

Do not gaze at wine when it is red, when it sparkles in the cup, when it goes down smoothly! In the end it bites like a snake and poisons like a viper. Your eyes will see strange sights and your mind imagine confusing things. You will be like one sleeping on the high seas, lying on top of the rigging. 'They hit me' you will say 'but I'm not hurt! They beat me, but I don't feel it! When will I wake up so I can find another drink?' - Proverbs 23

The day I knew those things was the day I graduated from CR.

I had overcome the hurdle of blindness to see myself clearly for who I was. In its place, a peaceful acceptance emerged. When I talked to people, I really listened instead of cutting them off with my own opinion and quick fix. My change became evident, and I was put back into leadership, but by this point, I viewed it as serving and not leading and took no pride in my position.

And yet, in spite of this growth, I forgot where I had come from—that I had touched hell and had been brought back. I forgot I had been leading my life straight into dangerous waters but was pulled out and placed on firm ground. After everything I had been granted, I fell into a period of resentment as I realized my life was not my own anymore to do whatever I wanted.

I went to Geneva on a business trip and decided to go to Paris and then take a train into Belgium. It seemed everyone in Paris smoked, and I was suddenly swept up by the glamor of it—as if I was missing out on something. I had never smoked before, nor had I ever desired to. But suddenly, all I could think about was how much I resented the fact I wasn't allowed to smoke.

As it turned out, the only available seat on the train to Belgium was in First Class in a smoking car. Before the train left the station, my eyes were stinging from the smoke. I was actually afraid I was not getting enough oxygen, so I left my cushioned seat in favor of a hard, fold-down seat in between cars. Even there the smoke was so dense it made me choke.

I laughed quietly to myself as I recognized God's hand in it all. I could hear Him say, "You want to smoke? Here. I'll let you smoke." How thoroughly and resoundingly cured I was of the desire after I went through that experience. But all things considered, I still hadn't surrendered my autonomy.

One morning two years later, I woke up mad and resentful. I didn't like the life I had anymore, and I was tired of being a goody-two-shoes. I just wanted to do what *I* wanted to do and lose myself in some dark and sultry bar with a hot guy. I stepped out of the subway into the winter sun and started walking towards work, full of rage.

That's it, God. I'm sick of sharing my faith, I said, my soul metaphorically raising its fist and shaking it at the heavens in defiance. *I'm not going to go to church anymore. And I'm done with reading the Bible.*

This internal rant was interrupted by a sharp whack on my head. I looked around, my hand feeling for the bump that was starting to form on my head, my mouth open in shock.

It was a ball of ice. From heaven.

I looked up, astonished, to see that more ice was falling from a skyscraper and bouncing off the sloped bottom of the building before flying all the way over to where I was. It was quite a distance as a small plaza separated the skyscraper from where I stood. It seemed odd because no one looked at me, or stopped, or seemed to notice there was something going on. It felt as if I had stepped out of time as I stood there like a stone, the current of humanity rushing past me.

God, did you just whack me on the head with a piece of ice? Because I was grumbling against you? I can NOT believe you just did that.

I cried all the way to work and cried at the office as I tried to tell my colleagues what had happened. I couldn't tell them what was really going on, that I was not crying from the pain, but rather from the stern discipline. It wasn't the bump on my head that hurt me the most. It was the fact I had actually gotten a whack on the head from the Lord Almighty—a divine spanking, so it seemed.

But as I grappled with it that day, my sore heart was slowly replaced with a gleam of understanding, followed by bubbling mirth.

God actually paid attention to me. He listened to what I was saying out of all the billions of people on the planet. I was stunned—and a bit awestruck—that He didn't allow me to get away with grumbling, which was to no one's benefit, and least of all to mine.

These hiccups in my faith revealed how foolish it was for me to cling to my autonomy and stubbornly pursue my selfish desires. I was learning that I was not immune to the consequences of my choices, not just in those moments of drunkenness but also in moments of folly. I believe the emphasis God was teaching me in those early days was not so much to be sober—but rather to have a more sober estimate of myself.

Have I not commanded you? Be strong and courageous. Do not be terrified; do not be discouraged, for the Lord your God will be with you wherever you go.
Joshua 1

10

A STAR-STUDDED SKY UPSIDE DOWN

There was a period of two years in 1997-1998 when I traveled back and forth to Asia as the newly promoted Director of Sales for the region, and if the soil of my heart had not already been thoroughly harrowed by divine discipline, the rigors of this lifestyle would certainly have done the trick. I was constantly jet-lagged, pushing my horizons, brushing off fatigue, in strange company, off-kilter in foreign cities, and alone for such long stretches of time there was little else to do but pray.

I traveled, on average, every six weeks for a spell of one to two weeks at a time. I went to almost every city in Asia, shoring up my considerable feelings of ease in the region. This position was not easy, and I did not wish to find another job in the same field when I was eventually laid off.

But for a time in my twenty-seven year old life, I had arrived. I wore suits with short skirts from Victoria Secret, quite fashionable at the time, and I had my own desk in a shared office with relative freedom as to when I came and left. When I entered the building, I walked past the glass room where Madonna took yoga classes. When I went out for lunch, I saw a harried Meg Ryan crossing over to a boutique in SoHo, hidden behind her large sunglasses. I clutched my briefcase to my side and took my place in the motley crowd.

I was playing a part. I neither understood finance, nor was I a shark, willing to do anything to make a sale. I didn't let on that I was out of my element when I sat with the Finance Minister of Thailand as he detailed his country's macroeconomics for me; I followed his discourse through a thick veil of incomprehension. But I claimed the position, enjoyed its perks, and faked my way through the rest.

When the Asian economy started to fold in 1998, leading to the eventual loss of my job, I finally understood that I had been coasting on the newspaper's reputation. The economy was rich, and sales came in without my having to work for them. But there came a point when nothing else was forthcoming, and I found myself sitting across from the Central Bank Governor of some emerging market country as he shrugged his shoulders and asked, "What should I do? Buy your company profile or provide food for my people?" The demise of my position was not long in coming after that.

But for those two years, I lived in a tired state of wonder, gaining experience beyond what I could have imagined. I stayed in nice hotels with spa-like bathrooms, tiled in beige, which afforded the most luxurious showers I've ever taken. I took cabs everywhere, ate in restaurants, and expensed it all. I filled my suitcase with samples of the newspaper, business cards, media kits, and business suits, and I packed quickly before each trip, a blasé routine born of habit and calm assurance.

Sometimes the countries were inviting places to visit, and I knew to expect an excellent level of English and attention to comfort. In Singapore, I stayed at the Holiday Inn on the Park, where I slept off my jet lag in the king-sized bed with crisp cotton sheets and a heavy white duvet. In the morning, I sat at the desk in a monogrammed cotton bathrobe, staring contentedly at the trees outside the window as I ate my breakfast in solitude, pouring strong hot coffee from the silver carafe. As the week wore on, and the jet lag shrugged off, I swam laps in the rooftop pool before the day began, dressing in the cool air conditioning before facing a day full of business meetings in the heat.

On these trips, I was usually alone and relied on my smile, a few rehearsed sales pitches, and the reputation of the newspaper to conduct business. I had plenty of time to think as I stared numbly at the scenes that flew by from my taxi window, always rushing from one meeting to the next, coming to life again as I was ushered into an elegant conference room. Fatigue was offset by privilege, and this façade gave me pleasure for some time.

Each country was different enough for me to appreciate its subtleties. In Tokyo, I took the director's business card with two hands, studied it, and asked questions about his position before putting it on the table as was expected. In Taipei, I found the clerks sleeping at their desks if I attended a meeting during lunch hour, but I was used to that and happy to be back in a country I knew so well. In Shanghai, I strolled through the old city after my workday was done, finding romance in the architecture and scouting a place to eat amid the warm lights and delicious smells floating in the air. The fragrant spices emanating from the restaurants were familiar to me from my two years in Taiwan, and I felt at home.

I also discovered cultures that were less familiar to me, and I faced them with a mix of eagerness and apprehension. When an upcoming trip to Pakistan was proposed, it jostled to my awareness a deep-rooted prejudice I had against Muslims, particularly Muslim men—I, who thought I had no prejudice at all. I was not only frightened to go because of how I might be treated, I was disdainful about what goodness and beauty I might find there. This revelation shocked me into prayer for God to remove such a prejudice from my heart.

On the next flight, I was seated next to a Muslim man who proudly showed me pictures of his wife and children, lovingly boasting about how perfect they were as he smiled at me then down at the picture. I smiled back at his friendliness and gentleness and was inwardly touched as his beautiful heart was revealed. There was no room for prejudice against this worthy soul, and the ugly weed was rooted out.

However, once in Pakistan, I knew not to stray outside the hotel, except in the company of the local consultant. I felt small, alone, and so white—so female—in this country. From the taxi, I eagerly looked around me, staring at the pale men of Karachi with their angular features, whose beard and hair were often henna-dyed red. When I later compared them to their compatriots further north who were thicker and swarthier, it was hard to believe these two peoples came from the same country.

Even the scenery was different with Karachi's sandy, desert-like aspect compared to the lush, verdant countryside that greeted me in Lahore. In the taxi ride from the airport to the city center, I drove past long stretches of bright green fields bordered by low-lying trees and rich clay roads leading to, I assumed, quiet villages tucked away. I stared at this fertile landscape, surreal in its beauty, and the chords of my chest thrummed as I imagined this must be what heaven looked like.

At the conclusion of my journey through Pakistan, I landed in the small, dark airport of Islamabad, a rude building surrounded by desert. At first glance, it seemed I was the only foreigner there. But when I looked to my right, I noticed a veiled Caucasian woman with washed-out, pale features and faded blue eyes. My heart leapt at finding, what I thought was, an American there by marriage. I longed to connect to her, but she completely ignored me.

As I was trying to place her, this woman who looked like me but was so clearly cloaked in foreign customs, I came to the conclusion that she must not be American. It was only later I made the connection that the Caucasus people, the ancestors to my own race, were also located in Afghanistan and had leaked out to the surrounding regions from there. This veiled woman who looked like me was home—but a home so removed from my own.

It wasn't just the religious variances that shook my narrow understanding of the world but also the governmental ones. I was required to engage a local business consultant in China because it would have been difficult to move freely on my own. She had a poor partner in me because I was more interested in courting adventure than landing the deal. She, herself, was driven—concerned with image, brand names, making money, and most importantly, landing the deal. I angered her when she lost face with a client by my refusing to try the deep-fried sea cockroaches he had ordered, and she scolded me roundly when we were on our own.

We communicated in a mixture of Chinese and English, and she cleared her throat constantly, a nervous tic that belied a fear of failure despite her hard edge. As we rode down a broad street on our way to a meeting in Beijing, I looked over and saw a long red brick wall, extending several blocks.

"What's that?" I asked her.

"It's Tiananmen," she answered, clearing her throat nervously.

"Wait. You mean Tiananmen Square? Where the massacre took place?" I was looking at her in astonishment, turning back to witness this site full of tragic history.

"Shh," she admonished me, glancing at the cab driver. "We don't talk about that here."

"But this is amazing. Did you know it was happening at the time?" I carried on, oblivious to her concern. I didn't understand that her life could be in danger if the taxi driver understood English and our talk was traced back to her. I couldn't fathom that in this post-Cold War age there could still be limits to free speech in a communist country, and along with it, repercussions.

She softened enough to say quietly, "It was not on the news, but we had friends in Singapore who told us it was happening. But we cannot talk about this," she emphasized again and turned her head towards the window, terminating the conversation.

In other countries, I was initiated into the difficulties of poverty and religious persecution. Whenever I could, I contacted the sister churches in the cities I was visiting, although in some places, Christians had been forced underground to avoid death or imprisonment.

Spending time with foreign brothers and sisters built my faith and gave me a breath of life after my solitude. In them I saw the same convictions, joy, and brotherhood I found in my home church. I also understood how simple life was in America, not just in our wealth, but also in our freedom.

In Jakarta, I invited the Women's Ministry Leader to dinner at my hotel. We spoke comfortably about our lives, and she mentioned the religious riots that had been occurring in the months prior—the persecution of Christians under certain Muslim sects. She told me that one Sunday they heard yelling and fighting growing louder near where their church service was being held. She stopped her story to take a bite of her dinner.

"What did you do?" I prompted her.

"We held our breath," she answered matter-of-factly. "The mob headed down our street, and we didn't make a sound. We were afraid for our lives. But then," she went on, "the noise eventually died down later in the day, and we saw that we were out of danger so we went home."

This matter-of-fact approach to difficulties seemed to be universal in this part of the world, yet there appeared to be no lack of joy in the midst of both persecution and poverty. I handed my passport to the Immigration clerk in Manila as I was arriving in the Philippines for the first time. He glanced at my passport, then stamped it and bid me a cheerful, "Happy Birthday." I was touched—and taken aback—as I thought, *This is the most welcoming of countries where they wish strangers a happy birthday.* But I discovered, as my taxi took me by the children playing and laughing outside their homes on the towering garbage heap, that their joy was born of hardship, and many were wreathed in smiles while living in abject poverty.

On one visit to Manila, I decided to stay an extra night with some of the sisters in their apartment instead of paying for a hotel. I had already gotten to know them on previous trips, and they made me feel welcome to come stay in their home.

That night I slept on a mattress on the floor with two other women in the same room. There were three more on the living room floor of the small apartment. Their front door was half-eaten by termites, so you could see people's legs as they walked along the corridor. One of the roommates could only pay her share of the rent and food by doing all the cleaning and cooking. She was too poor to contribute in any other way. The next morning, we all got up early to pray together— two of them in Tagalog, the only language they knew. I was impressed by their cheerful industry, and it didn't take many visits to fall in love with the Filipino people.

On my trip to India, I was invited to assist the Women's Ministry Leader by sitting in a study with an older woman whose sons had left the Hindu faith to become Christians. The mother was close to making the leap herself despite angry opposition from her husband. The minister asked her, "Are you willing to die for your faith?" At this time, the threats in India were growing against the Christians. She went on, "Are you willing to see your sons die for their faith?" The woman humbly murmured, "Yes, yes," in response to these questions.

I was shocked that someone should have to face such a thing in a country where Christianity was not officially illegal. Then the minister said, "Your husband is against your becoming a Christian. What if he locks you out of the house? What if you cannot return to your home?" Apparently, this was the risk others had faced who had gone before her.

The woman answered, "He cannot lock me out. We don't have a door."

It took us both a minute to process what the woman said. This family was so poor their house didn't even have a front door that could be closed and locked. Without a front door, there was no threat of her being locked out. All three of us burst into laughter at this upside to extreme poverty.

My faith was growing from the different challenges I encountered country to country, but it was also tried in intimate ways by forcing me to face the embarrassing phobia I'd had since I was little—a phobia so humiliating I wasn't even able to voice it until I was nearly thirty.

It all started out innocently enough. I was in elementary school, and our family was sitting in the pew at church one day when I asked my mom if I could go to the bathroom. She said no because the service was about to end. But I thought, *You mean...I might be in a place where I have to go the bathroom and I can't? But what if I have to?* This event launched a yearlong period of compulsive behavior where I constantly went to the bathroom in case I would later find myself in a place where there was none.

I overcame this habit, but when I was fifteen, I started having stomach problems related to what I now know is celiac disease—gluten intolerance. I was constantly at the pediatrician's who put me on diets of bread and Pepto-Bismol, alternating with apples and prunes in a span of three days each, which proved to be an unhappy formula. Over time, I mostly managed the stomach problems with a whole foods diet when under stress, but the secret phobia never left. When placed in situations where the problem kicked in, I had nothing to rely on except my faith. My trips abroad were a disaster waiting to happen, mixing bathroom phobias, third world countries, and a nervous stomach.

Oh dear, talk about having faith in the mundane. Talk about the foolish, the embarrassing, the—well, prayers don't get any more ridiculous than this—need for faith. Yet when emergency struck, I found myself sweating and praying desperately, "God please help me to hold on until I can make it to a bathroom." When you are that vulnerable, and I almost think you can't be more vulnerable except for when giving birth, desperation kicks in and you just lower your pride and ring your appeal out to the heavens.

In India, I was sitting in a hot cab, completely stationary because of a traffic jam and surrounded by beggars pawing at the car on all sides, when the sweaty cramps of the travel stomach began to kick in. I was on my way to an important meeting that could not be rescheduled, but I was forced to ask the cab driver to turn around and go back to the hotel. I prayed that God would bind my stomach, that He would clear the traffic jam so I would make it in time. He did. He did it every time. It's funny how faith can be built by human weakness, but mine really was.

I was stretched in courage and faith time and time again. I had made it to the Mumbai airport at three o'clock in the morning for my flight, after dragging myself from a sound sleep into the shower, then into a taxi racing to the airport through the black, deserted streets of the countryside. When I arrived, the place was in tumult, with hordes of people clamoring to be heard and shoving their tickets in the agents' faces. I waited patiently to the side until someone noticed me, a foreigner.

"Yes, I'm here for the flight leaving to London?" I said optimistically.

"Did you confirm your booking while in India?"

"No," I said, crestfallen. "I didn't know I needed to do that."

"Ma'am, we're so overbooked. I don't see how we're going to be able to get you on the plane."

On that particular trip I had been burrowing into the Charles Dickens's novel *Martin Chuzzlewit* and was drawing spiritual lessons from it. I was inspired by the attitude of the secondary character, who had decided he would cheerfully take whatever life handed him, determined to make the best of it. Despite the fact that I was exhausted and so ready to go home, with what seemed like both a bladder infection and an upset stomach kicking in, I decided to do the same. I answered the agent with a smile. "Just do what you can."

She bit her lip. "What's your final destination?" I told her that it was New York and she said, "Let me see what I can do."

Five minutes later, she solved the problem by bumping me up to First Class where I sat next to a tanned white man with an Indian accent and learned that there were still generations of British families with Indian citizenship who didn't leave after the war for independence. Although I wasn't able to enjoy the First Class fare because of my upset stomach, I was acutely sensible of God's kindness towards me.

Sometimes I traveled for a World or Development Bank Meeting instead of a sales trip, and this meant I was surrounded by familiar people—the editorial and journalistic staff from New York. On the last day of the Asian Development Bank meeting in Fukuoka, Japan, we had the afternoon to ourselves before flying out the next morning. I was exhausted from a week of intense conferencing and decided to wander off alone on the near-deserted beach. I kicked my shoes off and waded into the shallow water, soaking in the gray sky of the horizon far away and the soft sounds of water lapping against the shore behind me. With so few people nearby, I decided to pray then sing softly so no one would hear me.

It started to rain, and the few people on the beach fled for cover. I glanced around and saw I was alone, so I started to sing more loudly, daring myself to throw up my hands and praise God. I blushed at my audacity, feeling like an utter fool. But then I figured I may as well praise Jesus too, thinking it was about time I mentioned Him in more ways than just to terminate a prayer. It was difficult for me to say Jesus' name out loud, even though I believed in what He promised.

You see, I was just never a "Jesus" person. God I could do. God is easy. You say God and it's all-encompassing. There might be some other names, like Allah or Jehovah, but you're still on the same wavelength as the majority of the world. But the minute you use Jesus' name, you put yourself on a narrower path because He was the only one who claimed to be "the way to God." My whole being revolted at the idea of limiting myself to Jesus because I was afraid it meant I would become narrow-minded.

But on the day I dared to say Jesus' name out loud (just a whisper at first and then increasing in volume) something in me clicked. I realized that Jesus never said I had to be divisive and judgmental—He never asked that of me, and in fact, taught the opposite. He just asked for my love, which was something I could do even if it was given rather sheepishly at first.

Standing alone in the shallow waters of Fukuoka beach, I broke through my reserve for the first time and praised Jesus in public solitude. I caught a brief, virulent fever for my efforts and missed that night's closing revelry, but woke up the next morning fresh and alert for our flight back. I tucked the memory into my heart of the time I sang in the rain and overcame prejudice in my own faith.

There were so many long flights, and I remained silent, frightened by the turbulence, only opening my mouth to order dinner. I traveled bleary-eyed and awake. As the months wore on and I flew so often, I eventually learned to surrender my destiny and fall sleep on the plane.

I watched the sun rise on the clouds, the beam of morning sunlight reflecting off the wings and blinding me with its light. I saw the frightening nighttime thunderstorms below me, with lightening shooting off silently in different directions. I heard the flight attendant announce that we were not permitted to take pictures while we flew over Russia as I stared below at the bleak snowy tundra of Siberia.

One night towards the end of my period of travels, I was on my way into Singapore. We were nearly an hour away from our destination, and I was lost in the dark sky, the stars, and my faded reflection as I leaned my forehead against the cold window and looked down into the darkness.

Suddenly, I noticed white lights below me. At first it was just a light here and there, which made me think they were houses lost in the vast countryside. But then I realized that Singapore was an island—or at least, a series of islands—so these couldn't be lights from houses I was seeing. Where could they possibly be coming from?

We flew on, and as I started to see more and more lights appear below me, I became convinced that these had to be lights from fishing boats. There were so many of them, and so far apart, even when viewed from high altitude. I looked on in wonder, imagining what it must be like to be so far away at sea, you're surrounded by black water and nothing else. Eventually the boats appeared closer together, and as we descended, I started to see details like strings of lights on the sails, giving these massive vessels the appearance of charming toy sailboats.

But far, far up, with just the darkness above and below me, I stared down at the boats that were lost and isolated in the vast obscurity of the ocean, and whose lights were visible only to me. It struck me as I contemplated this star-studded sky upside down that this must be the way God sees His people who love goodness and mercy. We are the bright, shining lights He sees in a dark world, ravaged by evil and decay.

Keep me as the apple of your eye; hide me in the shadow of your wings.
Psalm 17

11

SPINNING DIZZILY

Being let go from my job was like taking a dip in the ocean in January with the Polar Bear Club. It was exhilarating to be free of a position that had become burdensome and to have the prospect of a new start before me, but my pride and self-esteem were doused in ice water and I was left spluttering. I studied the new manager as he tried to break the news gently, his language couched in compassion that was not inherent to him.

"So uh, should I work the rest of the day or am I just supposed to get my things and go?" My face felt hot with humiliation, although the news had not come as a complete surprise.

"You can just get your things and go." He gave a tight smile before turning towards the door.

One of the perks of being let go was that my commission was paid in full right away when it wasn't likely that the company would ever recover the advertising debt that some Asian banks had incurred following the crisis. Another perk of losing my job was that this was no longer my problem.

I took a deep breath and started to walk uptown, feeling strangely light-hearted despite the sting to my pride. Ignoring my heavy bag and the absence of a steady income, I wandered into Ann Taylor Loft. I tried on a few clothes, enjoying the near-empty store at mid-morning, and attempted to embrace freedom from routine. But eventually the store left me feeling dejected and I headed home.

At the time, I was living with two roommates, Neyra and Sue, in a luxury, high-rise apartment on the corner of Ninety-First Street and First Avenue. Neyra had a job with flexible hours, and she looked up in surprise when I opened the front door. "What are you doing here?"

"I got fired," I said, laughing, trying to make light of the situation but unable to stop the tears from falling. I sank down on the couch next to her and covered my face with my hands.

The following Monday, I plunged into the search for a new job. I had decided to look for something easy and routine, like a secretary position or a similar post with eight-hour days. Beyond that, I didn't have any clear idea of what I was looking for. The economy was less favorable than during my last job search, but I was naive enough to assume I would get a job in no time.

The agency sent me to a boutique bank on Fifty-Second Street—right around the corner from my old job. Someone led me to the conference room where my seat faced the hallway through the glass doors. The atmosphere in the office felt oppressive, and the people seemed dull. I thought, *there's no way I'm ever going to accept a job here.*

When I was given a tour of the bank, they showed me the desk I would be occupying, which faced the elevator. There was a quiet murmur as people conferred with one another or sat at their desks typing—so different from the lively atmosphere I had just left. The bank director seemed pleased as he looked over my skills and tested my level of Chinese with one of the employees. But I was sure it was a wrong fit for me. I had high aspirations. I was used to adventure—I was destined for something greater.

I needed a job, but didn't really want *that* job so I decided to pray for specifics that would make God's will clear. I was willing to let prayer determine my path and obey the call when the prayers were answered. But my plan was to offer prayers that would make it too difficult for God to answer, thereby preventing Him from approving a position I didn't want. I prayed that in the second interview the director would offer to pay for my continuing education without me bringing the subject up.

However, in the second interview the director said, "The agency told me you would like to continue your studies." I nodded. He paused for a moment before looking up from my resumé and saying, "We would pay for that."

I was astonished that this prayer was answered so succinctly, but even that was not enough for me. If I was going to be serving people coffee every day, I had to be sure this was the right fit. So I also prayed that if this was the job for me, they would call me the next day with an offer, and that they would propose ten thousand dollars more than what I had been making as a Regional Director.

The next day, five o'clock came and went; six o'clock came and went. I thought—that's it. God has made it clear this is not the place for me. The workday has ended, and I didn't get the offer today. Phew.

At six-thirty, the agency called and said the bank wanted to make me an offer of thirty-eight thousand dollars, plus a guaranteed bonus of two thousand dollars.

I hesitated, as I processed the fact that only half of my prayer was answered. They weren't offering the base salary I had prayed about. "I'm not interested in the job for that salary," I replied and then told her what I was asking.

She digested this, before replying scornfully, "But you *will* be getting that amount if you include the bonus, and it's still way more than what you were making in your last job. And they're willing to pay for your education."

But I remained firm. "I'm sorry. I'm not willing to accept the job for that amount." The agent all but slammed the phone down on me.

I was self-satisfied at first; after all, I hadn't wanted the job. But then I started to feel pressure from the fact that nothing else was forthcoming, and I did have to earn money at some point. Then I started to get insecure, thinking that everything the agent said was true. I was a fool to turn down such a good offer when I wasn't sure I would get another one. I started to repent of my fastidiousness in having turned it down. The next day, the agent called back to ask, "If the base salary is forty thousand, will you take it?"

"Yes," I said without hesitation.

"Well you've got yourself a job then. I can't believe he came up to your price, but he did."

So I started my job with fresh enthusiasm and with the proper dose of gratitude.

My new title was Executive Assistant, Assistant in Human Resources. Ironically, as much as I had been certain the position was not for me, I was really happy there. I was able to have peace and quiet and an easy rhythm that went on comfortably until five o'clock each day. I found that I liked crunching numbers in payroll and that I was good at editing and drafting letters. I found pleasure in organizing the files and ticking off my manageable to-do list each day. I also got along well with my immediate boss. I don't think I've ever had such a span of time where everything fit so neatly into place—in work, as in life.

I was happy in my home-life too. I had a stable living situation with roommates who made up a tight family to counter the loneliness of living in a large city. We always had friends coming and going, breathing a lively, cheerful air into our apartment.

My roommate Sue was Korean-American with large doe-like eyes, a tender heart, and a no-nonsense approach to life. Neyra was Puerto-Rican, and her intense suffering as a child had transformed her into a worldly-wise, laid-back woman with a deep, infectious laugh. We made sure to have a "family night" once a week where we made dinner and rented a movie or went out.

"Jen*nie*!" Sue welcomed me as I walked in the door after midweek, accenting the last syllable in that dulcet voice of hers. "Just be his *friend*," stressed Neyra whenever I rhapsodized over my latest crush as we sat cross-legged, eating lime-flavored tortilla chips. Neyra and Sue each had a boyfriend, but I had only my crushes, and I put my head in the clouds every time I lost my heart. Neyra deemed it her affectionate duty to put my feet back on the ground.

Neyra also set me up with Matthieu.

I had spoken to Matthieu before. I knew he had been baptized around the same time I had and that we had some good friends in common. We had a few brief encounters, but instead of piquing my interest, these only served to make me dislike him. Our first conversation was when I bounded up to him at church and told him I spoke French, confident he would be impressed. But he didn't smile at all; he just nodded his head and muttered a reply. That quickly deflated my generosity, and I thought he was rather haughty for someone so skinny.

Over the years a few different people said things like, "I know someone you would totally like," or "I know just the person you should get to know better—you have so much in common." As soon as the name Matthieu cropped up, I stopped listening.

Once, and I can only vaguely call up the memory after José reminded me of it, I spontaneously grabbed his arm and asked, "José, where's my future husband? Who am I going to marry?"

Matthieu was crossing our path at that instant, and José pointed and said, "Him." He had gone white-water rafting with Matthieu a few weeks earlier and had joined the ranks of the enthusiasts in aligning our future.

"Hm. Mm," I shook my head. "Come on. You know he's not my type."

Our church had the culture of greeting each other with a hug—you know, the casual across the back type of thing. Once I found myself standing right next to Matthieu at church. We smiled at each other, and he gave me a hug.

It was such a good hug. It wasn't wimpy like I thought it would be, him being so skinny and all. It was friendly, firm, and welcoming. I was taken aback as it occurred to me that he was both warmer and more confident than I expected. In a split-second, I considered the options. "If I started a conversation with him he would probably ask me out on a date." But then I thought, *"Naa."* So I moved away and looked for other people I thought would be more interesting.

Neyra spoke to Matthieu about me on a day he had just experienced a "disappointment" in his love life. I know this because he told me after we were married. He was standing at the sink washing dishes and brooding over his situation. Finally, he was inspired to pray, "God, not only do I not know what I need, I don't even know what I want. I pray that you find a wife for me."

When just a few short hours later, Neyra mentioned asking me on a date, he thought to himself, "Could this be the answer to my prayer? So soon?" But that would have been ridiculously immediate. "No, no—it can't possibly be," he thought.

When he didn't call, Neyra reminded him about asking me out, but it was as if any sense of immediacy was blunted. He had some vague thought of, "Oh yeah, I need to call her like I said I would." But he wasn't sure who I was and wasn't motivated to go on another blind date.

One day, things changed when I saw a mass e-mail with mutual friends, and his name was on the list of recipients. I couldn't miss it—it was the only one all in capital letters. His name stood out from the rest like it was heralding the presence of a prince among the court.

Without thinking twice, I copied his address and pasted it into a fresh e-mail, and wrote,

"Hi Matthieu,

I'm friends with Betsy and roommates with Neyra and everyone tells me you're a great friend to have. We should hang out sometime.

Jennie"

If I had liked him I wouldn't have had the courage to do this, but as it stood, I had nothing to lose. He lost no time in writing back and setting something up. He also let on that he wasn't sure who I was, so I told him that I was the one who spoke French.

That called up a vision of me in a moment of awkwardness, he later told me. He was sitting with a friend at a diner, and he watched as I came in and was hailed by a large group sitting at a nearby table. I looked a little out of place with them, blushing, and unsure of where to sit. And he thought to himself, "Aw, I'll be your friend." This is what he remembered about me when he realized who I was.

The night we went out, I wore tall black boots with a knee-length circle skirt and a crimson top. I was excited for the date, even though I wasn't expecting anything more than friendship. He picked me up at the door, greeted Neyra and Sue, then smiled at me as we waited nervously by the elevator. He was friendlier than I thought he would be.

As we were crossing the street to head towards the subway, he put his hand on my arm and said, "No, it's this way." I looked at him blankly.

"My car. It's over here," he explained, smiling.

I couldn't believe I was going on a date with a man who had a car—in *Manhattan*. He opened the door for me and waited until I settled into the leather seat before walking around and getting into the driver's side. My nerves were bouncing up and down.

We went to a teahouse first, which gave us a chance for quiet conversation. As we talked, I had a fleeting thought that he almost perfectly matched what I had been praying for in a husband—a man who loved children and classical music, was from a different country, and spoke a different language. But the man I had been praying for would have black curly hair and Matthieu's hair was red. He was going to be my friend.

Eventually we walked across the street from the teahouse and met a group of friends for dinner. Even though there were many people whom we both knew, we were still wrapped in our own conversation as we ate. After dinner, salsa music started playing, and Matthieu lifted his eyebrows. "Shall we dance?"

"Sure," I answered nervously. I was not one to say no. But I had no idea how to dance salsa, or how I was supposed to dance it with him, or whether he even knew what he was doing. But it seemed like he *did* know because he led me confidently to the middle of the dance floor. As I stood there, my eyes frozen wide and my mouth slightly open in panic, he sashayed his way over to me and grabbed my hands.

"Holy coooow," I whispered to myself, giggling as he grabbed me with firm hands and sure feet and swept me into the turns.

"Here, hold your arms firm like this," he said as he showed me, his feet unable to stay still when the music was pulsing. I laughed nervously, unable to take the stupid grin off my face. He didn't seem to notice my awkwardness and kept adjusting his steps to compensate for my own that were faltering.

After a short time under his guidance, I was starting to follow more smoothly. It didn't seem as if he would ever tire, and every so often, he glanced at me and smiled encouragingly as I focused on not making a mistake. I forgot we were supposed to be friends when he held me like that. When his hands grabbed me around the waist and then spun me away, my stomach quivered in a way that didn't feel like we were friends. Instead, this man who was "not my type" was inexplicably causing my heart to fall into my stomach in a strange way. When the evening was over, I could barely see my way off the dance floor because of the stars in my eyes.

I knew Neyra would be seeing him at her midweek service that Tuesday, so I made him a thank-you card and a small batch of Indian samosas, a nod to the fact that I remembered he had also traveled to India for his job. I was excited for her to tell me all about their conversation—to find out what he thought of me.

"So?" I asked excitedly, a silly grin plastered on my face as soon as she walked through the door. "Did he like the samosas? Did he have a good time on our date?" I peppered her eagerly.

"No," she said firmly, shaking her head.

"Wait...what? He didn't like the samosas? Or he didn't like me?"

She continued to look at me, her expression serious and resolute.

I couldn't believe it. My face fell as I was overcome by the sensation that my entire future was being stolen from me. There was no way...I knew this guy. He had to have felt the same way about me that I felt about him. My expression took on tragic proportions.

"Ha. Gotcha!" Neyra said laughing at me as I sat down feebly. "He had a great time."

"But *just—be—his—friend*," she stressed with her twinkling grin.

Sometimes God gives you a respite from the hardships and pressures of life so He can shower you with blessings. You hold firmly to the roundabout and run and run with the other children until you can't keep up any longer. You throw yourself onto the roundabout as it whirls around and around. The scenery whips by in a blur and you sit and watch it, feeling gravity tug deliciously at your core. Before long, the panorama starts to slow down until you are able to notice the trees glinting in the sun, the sand on the playground, the small insects darting here and there in the sunlight. You feel the fresh breeze on your skin, and you keep turning around and around, slower now, but without any effort at all.

This was that period of blessing for me—and I was spinning dizzily.

"I clothed you with an embroidered dress and put sandals of fine leather on you. I dressed you in fine linen and covered you with costly garments. I adorned you with jewelry: I put bracelets on your arms and a necklace around your neck, and I put a ring on your nose, earrings on your ears and a beautiful crown on your head. So you were adorned with gold and silver; your clothes were of fine linen and costly fabric and embroidered cloth. Your food was honey, olive oil and the finest flour. You became very beautiful and rose to be a queen. And your fame spread among the nations on account of your beauty, because the splendor I had given you made your beauty perfect," declares the Sovereign Lord. Ezekiel 16

12

CHOSEN

I stretched on the low wall that bordered the entrance to the reservoir in Central Park, waiting until there was a lull in the joggers running past before taking my place in the stream of people. Propelled by hope and fresh air, I ran quickly and lightly, my breath barely accelerating as I rounded the West Side of the circuit. I didn't always bother with music when I ran; I was just happy to listen to the birds along the shady path, to look at the trees in full bloom, and to let my thoughts wander. It was Friday, and my one-year anniversary with Matthieu.

I thought about the brief e-mail Betsy had sent me a few weeks ago, which set my hopes up regarding my future with Matthieu: "Tell me exactly what kind of ring you want and what size you are. Inquiring minds want to know."

I immediately ran down the street and got sized at Cartier's, but after sending her five e-mails in one hour, she finally responded, "Sorry to disappoint you Jen, but I don't know anything. I just wanted to know what kind of ring you wanted."

What kind of ring was easy. When I first moved to New York, one of my co-workers got engaged. This was when I had broken up with Olivier and was feeling especially forlorn. She came in one day wearing a solitaire one-carat diamond, framed by two small baguette diamonds, all set in platinum.

What a beautiful ring, I thought, as I looked at her beaming face. *I wish somebody loved me enough to give me a ring as pretty as that.* This was the ring I described to Betsy, even though I didn't have much hope of getting anything so costly—even though I knew I was hopelessly shallow.

I finished my second lap around the reservoir and turned on to Eighty-Ninth Street, where I walked along the tree-lined sidewalk that held rows of brownstone apartments. The men selling bagels were setting up their stands on the street corner, and I could smell coffee when I walked by. As I approached Lexington Avenue, I heard the hiss of the bus as it opened its doors and the honking of taxis as they rushed by. The city was coming to life.

Neyra, Sue, and I were now living in a different apartment down the street from our former building. There were four of us now to counter the increased amount in rent. Lisa was our new roommate, a musician from Minnesota who had spent a year on a kibbutz in Israel. At home, I showered and put on perfume then dressed in my grey pants, black cardigan, and platform shoes that made a nice clicking sound when I walked. I didn't stay for breakfast as I was craving the moist cappuccino muffins near my office. I grabbed my small patent-leather backpack, yelled goodbye to my roommates and walked out the door.

At work, I swiveled in the chair as I set up my station, chatting with my colleague, JoAnne. She was the one who had set the bouquet of flowers on my desk the day Matthieu took me to Central Park for a picnic lunch date and asked me to date him exclusively. We walked back to my office, hand in hand, and when I took the elevator up to my floor, I saw JoAnne peering at me from her desk, before glancing at the flowers. "He must have been confident you would go out with him." I nodded, grinning.

As my computer slowly flickered to life, I had a chance to reflect on our year together. I had learned to let him take the first steps—to e-mail and call first, to set up dates and worry about the details. But I was always smilingly consistent—I would not be the one to break his heart.

I felt the same reassuring presence from him. He always greeted me with a warm smile, and singled-out attention that showed me I was the only one who mattered. When we had been dating for only a short time and were seated at an indoor garden for lunch, he told me he had just found out his visa might be denied. He might be forced to go back to France.

My appetite left me, and I remembered what the lack of visa had done to my last relationship, even if it was a different affair and a completely different man. My visa had expired, and I was forced to go home with no one to claim me and ask me to stay.

But Matthieu put his hand over mine and coaxed my eyes up to his, saying, "This has nothing to do with you and me. No matter what happens with the visa, I'm not going anywhere." My heart flooded with warmth and security.

We had serious talks about commitment while keeping our relationship completely pure. Neither of us was a virgin, but we weren't having sex, and people who didn't share our faith thought we were crazy. "Wait, you mean you're not going to have sex with the guy until you marry him? But what if the sex is really bad? You'll be stuck with him for life."

I wasn't worried about that, given our level of attraction, and I didn't mind when people said those sorts of things either. Although at one time I would have found the idea crazy too, it had become natural when I saw everyone else in our church managing to do that very thing. They were young and attractive; they were confident and successful. If they could talk about purity openly and put it into practice as they followed God, so could we.

Purity in relationships came with being part of this church, and I agreed to the "church pressure" about obeying the Bible in this area. At first I was going along in blind obedience, but it wasn't until I actually lived it out that I started to see why something like that might be beneficial. Without the physical aspect, our friendship deepened and metamorphosed slowly.

This was one of the ways we learned to love and respect one another before ever having to vow that we would. When I went by swinging my hips in my new pale-blue skirt with little cherry blossoms (confident that I was a walking vision of loveliness), Matthieu didn't tell me how pretty I was in my new outfit; instead he asked me to change.

"Um," he hemmed uncomfortably, "Could you please not wear skirts? Ever? Or, if you do wear skirts, could they be, like, down to your ankles?" I hadn't understood what a trigger bare legs could be for a man, especially when they were brushing up against his.

The adjustment period went both ways. "I'm not going to eat sugar any more," I declared one day. "It's really bad for me—it makes my blood sugar go all over the place." It took only a short time for my resolve to crumble as I helped myself to a cookie in front of him a few days later.

"But...I thought you said you couldn't eat sugar anymore," he said, shocked.

"Oh, that. It's not that big a deal. Besides I wanted it," I said, shrugging my shoulders.

He looked at me in disbelief. "I don't think I can go out with someone like you," was all he could manage, unable to articulate the horror he felt over my lack of character.

"What?" I said, nearly laughing. "Don't give up on me already. It's not like you don't have any faults of your own," I exclaimed indignantly. He needed some time to process my weaknesses, and didn't appreciate my reminding him of his. However, with time, the more I let him into my life full of inconsistencies and weaknesses, the more he was able to show me grace. And that worked both ways.

I was forced to tell him about my depression—something I hadn't been particularly trying to hide, but which I considered a thing of the past. Yet for reasons I couldn't understand, it was during this happy period of my life that I needed to start taking anti-depressants again. I had a safe, pleasant living situation, a stable, rhythmic job, and I had fallen in love with a great guy. Yet I began to experience debilitating anxiety and depression and began taking Prozac again under medical supervision.

We were learning to change and mold to each other's spirit—I in respecting him and responding with more humility and gentleness—and he in showing me more grace. Through our fights and struggles, and even through the physical barrier we put up between ourselves, our spirits meshed together naturally and gradually. Our heartstrings interwove with iron bonds.

It was a strange feeling to be attracted to one another and not act on it. At times it was a struggle, and we couldn't even hold hands without noticing it. Other times it felt like we were just friends, and I was almost afraid we had lost the attraction completely. But we couldn't be sure when the playful friendship would suddenly turn into something else, so we were careful to keep temptations to a minimum. We didn't spend any time alone behind closed doors, and we limited our kisses to a peck on the lips. We greeted each other with a hug and kiss, and said goodbye the same way. Well...we also had what we called the "swing kiss"—that impromptu kiss that might occur at any point during the date. I liked the swing kiss.

Although I hadn't found Matthieu handsome in the beginning, I always wanted to stand next to him, to be as close to him as I could, to spend as much time together as possible. Then one day, the veil over my eyes lifted.

I looked up at his green eyes and square jaw, and my mouth opened a little. "Wh...when did you get so cute?" We were standing at the crosswalk, arm in arm, and he stared down at my upturned face for a minute before suddenly leaning down and planting a kiss fully on my mouth. My heart fluttered and I looked at him in confusion.

Then he looked ahead, smiling, as the light changed. "That was our swing kiss," he said, pulling me across the street.

Purity healed things I wasn't even aware were broken. We celebrated his birthday by organizing a huge party at his apartment. I was setting out the food with his roommates, discussing last-minute details on the theme. I took my sweater off as I worked, revealing the tight jeans and close-fitted top I had on underneath. He went into the bedroom for a minute to compose himself, and when he came back out, he looked awkward as he quietly asked, "I'm so sorry, but could you please put your sweater back on?"

The floor opened up before me, a yawning pit, as I realized the implication of what he was saying. My face burned with the shame of not being good enough—of never being good enough. Here it was happening again, but this time coming from a man I trusted.

"It's because you think I look fat?" I asked in a faltering voice, already sure of the answer.

"Uh no," he said, laughing with surprise. "Quite the contrary," he added in a strangled voice.

I looked at him in amazement before reaching for my sweater. He didn't think I was fat. In fact, he was attracted to me exactly as I was. He wanted me to cover up because he didn't want to be too tempted—by me. Healing balm poured over my damaged soul. This balm covered every flaw and soothed my heart. I began to walk in beauty as I was made whole again and the damage of my past was undone.

There were parallels in our lives that both astonished me and made me feel I had been waiting for him my whole life. Matthieu had been an atheist before studying the Bible, so I asked him on our first date to tell me how he became a Christian. It was such a drastic change to undergo. I mean, I believed in God, even if it hadn't been a priority for me, but Matthieu hadn't even believed that God existed.

He told me how he arrived in New York City and knew no one, how he went to a jazz café with the sole intention of trying to make friends. That's where, for the first time in his entire life, he opened his mouth to make conversation with someone he hadn't been introduced to first.

The trumpet player's name was Brad, and he was going around with the hat for donations after his band finished playing. Matthieu asked if he knew of any group he could join to play saxophone. When Brad found out Matthieu was French, he called Jean-Jacques over, who managed the café, and they invited him to play at their next jam session. They also invited him to church.

"So my first service was the Sunday where there was Daylight's Savings Time..." Matthieu told me.

"That was my first time at church too," I interrupted. I knew we had been baptized around the same time, but I didn't know we had gone to church for the first time on the same day.

"I was an hour early because I didn't know about the time change," he continued.

"What? You're kidding. So was I," I interrupted again, pleased to find we had this connection. "So...when did you get baptized?"

"It was December 12th," he said. "I was leaving for Paris, and I was afraid not to be covered if anything happened to the plane, so I got baptized the morning before I left."

"I got baptized December 11th at night," I exclaimed. "We were just twelve hours apart." It seemed so coincidental that our faith journeys happened at the same time.

He went on to tell me about his first study where he learned about the Crucifixion. He said, "After we studied, Brad asked me how I felt, so I said I was scared. Then he asked me why. And I answered, 'Because I don't believe this is true, but I know that if it *is* true, I'm going to have to change my life.'"

As he talked about his evolution to faith, the dream I'd had when I was seventeen came flooding back, along with all the parallels in our story. So it had been prophetic after all, this dream I had of having a French husband—the dream I had dismissed after breaking up with Olivier.

We had been wandering in the dark of the forest together as we both stumbled and struggled in our former lives. We exited the forest into the bright light, hand in hand, as we claimed our lives again. Spiritually speaking, we went from dark to light together as we both made the decision to get baptized twelve hours apart. But we would never know our destiny was aligned until three years had passed.

How fretful I had been the night I decided not to get baptized, moaning to God about having to give up my boyfriend in order to follow Him. "I'll never find another one like him, and on top of it, he's French." All along, even down to the matching scars on our heads from a bike and car accident, God was preparing a match so perfect it could only have been divinely inspired.

As the year drew to a close, all I wanted was not to have to go home to separate houses anymore. I didn't want to have to say goodbye at the end of each date. I didn't want him to leave.

That night after work, Matthieu brought me to a French restaurant in SoHo that overlooked Broadway. We sat in the bay window, and I smiled at him over the white tablecloth and small candles.

At the beginning of the meal, he told me he had an anniversary present for me. I thought, *This is it.*

But he pulled out a long navy blue box. It was too long to be a wedding ring, and even though I still held on to hope before opening it, I felt my heart plunge in disappointment when I saw that it was a diamond chip tennis bracelet in white gold.

"Thank you," I said in surprise, with the ghost of a smile. "It's so pretty," I added, as I put it on.

It *was* pretty. I had never been given a nicer piece of jewelry in my life, but the ungrateful thought kept barging into my whirling brain that now it would take him forever to come up with enough money to buy me a proper engagement ring.

I tried to smile and hide my disappointment behind cheerful conversation, but the evening had lost its luster. The only thing that kept me going was a persistent glimmer of hope that maybe, just maybe, he would still ask me to marry him. Everything seemed to point towards it—the one-year anniversary, the French restaurant—I was so desperate to marry him, I would have even said "yes" without the ring.

So we ate the four-course meal with more silence between us than usual. Before dessert, I told him I needed to run to the ladies' room where I proceeded to cool my flushed cheeks with water from the sink. I stared at my face in the mirror, my hands on the counter, and tried to steady myself. Then I walked back across the restaurant towards Matthieu.

When I sat down, he opened his hands on the table to take mine and started by saying, "You know, I prayed for exactly what I wanted in a girlfriend."

"Me too," I said eagerly. "I prayed for a boyfriend who was strong spiritually, who loved children, and who was from a different country…" I trailed off, realizing how lame I sounded in my own ears.

He heard me out patiently and continued as if I hadn't interrupted him. "I prayed for a woman like you. You're beautiful," he said smiling. "You love God, you love children, you love music. You're everything I prayed for…and I decided that one year is just not good enough for me."

He pulled out a small square box and put it on the table. "I want to spend the rest of my life with you."

Everything stood still. I no longer heard the soft chatter of the other diners, or the cars passing by on the street outside our window. All I could see was him looking at me hopefully, confidently, as he opened the box with the ring—my dream ring—glittering and winking at me in the candlelight.

"Will you marry me?"

Place me like a seal over your heart, like a seal on your arm; for love is as strong as death, its jealousy unyielding as the grave. It burns like blazing fire, like a mighty flame. Many waters cannot quench love; rivers cannot wash it away. If one were to give all the wealth of his house for love, it would be utterly scorned. Song of Solomon 8

13

SEALED

"You raised the bar for all the other brothers, Matthew," Yvonne said in her reluctant drawl that made us want to laugh. They were standing in the cool night air of our outdoor garden, which was packed with people, hors d'oeuvres, and a sound system in the corner that gave off a cheerful beat.

"Now all the sistas are gonna say, 'I see the ring…but where's ma brace-let?'"

In my breathless excitement of being proposed to, I must have managed to squeak out a "yes" because Matthieu looked relieved, then excited. Then he made a surreptitious phone call, which brought my roommates into the restaurant two minutes later with broad smiles and bouquets of flowers. Matthieu paid for the check, and we piled into his car to head back uptown.

I knew something was up the minute I saw my roommates. Oh, and I suppose I suspected something when we all arrived at our home. But it was still a joyful shock to be greeted with an apartment crowded with friends, who had all kept the secret, yelling, "Congratulations," as soon as we walked in the door. There was no lull following my engagement.

Matthieu handed me off to my friends to spend the evening laughing, hugging, and showing off my ring. He carried on quiet conversations with people in the background, watching me as I flitted around, high from excitement. He only stepped in to tell me that my parents, whom he had called in advance to ask for their blessing, were waiting for my phone call.

The next day, as we sat down on the grass in Riverside Park to figure out when and where to hold the wedding, there was something different between us. There was a promise, anticipation, a barrier removed that allowed us to get even closer. As I looked into his eyes and smiled, I saw the same joy reflected back at me. We agreed on the small chapel at Columbia University as the location for the ceremony, to be set at the earliest possible date that could accommodate both families.

Matthieu loved the acoustics of the chapel, the way it gave golden timbers to the music that was played inside. He also thought the style of it would please his parents, who were both architects. I simply loved the chapel for its tall wooden doors that—once closed—you forgot about until they opened for the bride, ushering her in with long rays of sunshine.

I knew the dress I wanted. I couldn't have spent six months working for a top wedding gown designer while dating Olivier without dreaming of the dress I would choose when I married him. But I knew it was proper form to try on everything, because one never knows what suits until it's actually on. I was with my roommates and a few other friends, surrounded by mountains of dresses and brides in varying states of joy and stress, when, amid the racks, I saw it—my dress.

"This is the one," I said.

"Try it on, Jen," Neyra said, practically. "You don't know until you have it on."

The bodice was plain and strapless, with a thick seam of sequins and pearls underneath, which formed an empire waist. The rest of the dress was plain and fitted, cut only in an A-line towards the bottom to allow for the back of the dress to trail behind. The short train hooked on top between the shoulder blades. I stared in the mirror with satisfaction and walked out, my eyes sparkling.

"Yes, Jennie." "Oh that's it. That's the one." "It's perfect." My cheering squad confirmed my pick, only pausing to see if I would look better in ivory than in white. I didn't. I brought the dress over to the counter and reached in my bag to pull out my credit card.

"No, Jennie," said Neyra, scooting me out of the way as she opened her wallet. "This one's on us," as Sue and Lisa stood next to her smiling and nodding. My roommates paid for my wedding dress, and I didn't know how to process such a loving gesture.

Since there were ten bridesmaids in all shapes and sizes, I let them choose the dress they wanted, specifying only that I wished for them to wear long dresses in the color ruby-Bordeaux. That would make everyone's skin glow, from the palest Texan to the darkest Jamaican. I wanted them to be beautiful in the autumn leaves as we took our pictures after the ceremony.

We set the most important details in motion—dresses, the date, the church, and reception hall. Then we left for France to meet Matthieu's family. His brother was getting married two months before us, and this provided the perfect opportunity for Matthieu to bring his fiancée home before we all met again at our own wedding.

As soon as I stepped into their comfortable, solidly-built marble and cement house, covered in green vines, I was offered refreshments and promptly forgotten. Matthieu went downstairs to look through a few things, his mother invited me to lie down on the couch (which I did), and his father pulled out his saxophone and started playing jazz tunes while his brother sat down at the piano to accompany him. A spontaneous jam session.

I grew up in a house with music pouring out of every room. My father practiced his French horn in the kitchen, pausing only to yell at some stupid move a football player made in the game, my brother alternated between classical and jazz piano in the living room, and my mother listened to opera upstairs in the bedroom. I felt at ease in the informal bustle and noise, the complete lack of ceremony.

His brother's wedding was a sweet affair, set in the countryside where his bride was from. Their first glimpse of each other was when they each stumbled out of their family car in full dress, grinning shyly at each other, before going into the Town Hall for the civil ceremony.

Following that, we all drove over to the church for the religious ceremony where things unrolled more traditionally, including the entrance of the bride to the organ playing the wedding march.

The reception was held outdoors on a hot day. We took pictures in the green grass next to the pond, and ate our dinner in the covered open-air reception hall. There was a wheel of brie set out, as big as a small table, and couples started dancing the minute the food was cleared away. Matthieu and I danced carefully next to the swirling couples around us, mindful not to get too caught up in the romance of the situation. It was not our time yet. Then he brought me to the bed-and-breakfast where we would be staying, each in our own room.

Before returning to New York, we went to visit his family's country home near the cathedral of Chartres. We went with his mom, first to visit the cathedral, and then to the house where we aired out the rooms that had not been used in awhile. The stone house was part of an old hamlet comprising four other buildings in varying states of habitation. His mother had spent her summer vacations there, and her father lived out the latter days of his life in the home, producing paintings until he died.

The well was from the thirteenth century, and we had to duck under the doorframes because the hamlet was built when people were much smaller. It was a beautiful day, and we set out a picnic lunch of salad, cold cuts, bread, and cheese. Then we spent the afternoon with the rusty scythe and clippers, trimming as much of the grass and bushes as we could. I was so happy to be there, so happy to know my future in-laws, whose open acceptance showed promise of many peaceful years together.

Back in New York, things were starting to come to a head as we organized the details, and our friends pitched in to help. Kelly's gift was to design our programs and pluck my eyebrows into perfect arches. Kim made my veil and then missed the wedding ceremony so she could decorate the reception hall in white lights, tulle, and white candles. Rosalind made the dresses for my dancers and was my aide-de-camp, doing everything there was to do behind-the-scenes. I timidly approached Christianne and Sonja—beautiful, identical twins from our church who studied with the New York City Ballet—to ask if they would possibly dance at my wedding, and they graciously agreed. They were excellent dancers and very elegant; I knew they would provide exactly the pictorial image I had hoped for. I wanted them to be like…fairies—or wood nymphs—with white dresses and white flowers woven in their dark ringlets. And I wanted them to prepare the way for the bride, just like in a fairy tale. Josette heard I was using dancers for the ceremony and approached me with the offer to choreograph. "Oh yes," I said, "and I know just what I want."

My lingerie shower was the Thursday night before the wedding. It's certain I would have blushed rosily no matter what, but having my mother-in-law present, who had already arrived from France, made me feel all the more embarrassed as leather, padding, feathers, and silk came out of the wrappings, some of which I didn't even know what to do with. And then—flannel teddy-bear pajamas.

"You might get cold," my mother-in-law said as everybody laughed.

Stress poked holes in my happiness. The week before the wedding, my dress didn't fit. It hadn't really fit when I first got it, but I had two months left, and I was sure I would lose weight from excitement. There came a point, though, when I couldn't put off trying it on any longer, even though I was fairly certain my weight hadn't budged.

I tried the dress on and felt the blood drain from my face as I saw that I was unable to pull the zipper up. I gave up and collapsed on the couch in despair, which is where Neyra found me when she came home. "Jennie," she said, pointing to my room. "Go get your dress and put it on." I obeyed, sure my fears would be confirmed. She hooked the top of the dress and started yanking the zipper up the back. It wasn't budging easily, but by force of me sucking in my stomach, and her yanking the sides together to get the zipper up inch by inch, she got it all the way to the top. I looked like a sausage, but it had closed.

She came around to look at me critically from the front, and then started yanking my dress up and shoving some of the fabric under the seam of the bodice. Suddenly I could breathe again, and the dress fit snugly but not ridiculously. The bodice had just been too long, and it was an easy fix to shorten it until I could move again. I trembled with relief.

The morning of my wedding finally came. When my alarm went off at six o'clock, I shut it off and leaned on one elbow to peer out the window. It was a good sign that I didn't see any rain, although it was still too early to tell what the day held.

My colleagues had chided me a lot about the weather because the forecast called for ninety-five percent chance of rain. The odds were definitely not in favor of a dry, sunny autumn wedding. When they teased me, I always responded in the same way with a smile. "Oh, I'm sure God's going to give me some sun."

But inside I wasn't confident. I kept thinking about my vision, my dream of walking into the church with rays of sunlight at my back. I asked God to give me sun just for the moment when the doors opened for my entrance. That's all I was asking. This one issue didn't matter a bit in the scheme of the wedding, and yet it mattered to me. It was the whole reason I had wanted to get married in this church in the first place—because the entrance was so beautiful with rays of sun streaming in. *Won't you please do that for me? To show me that you're pleased with the wedding? I want to see your presence there.* I prayed.

I sprang out of bed and took extra care in taking a bath. Afterwards, I dressed in jeans and a button-down shirt. Then I put on a cardigan, threw my dress over my arm, and walked down the street to my old building. Genieve lived there and opened up her home to me and the other bridesmaids so we could all get ready together, cheerfully setting out coffee and muffins.

Carpio, Matthieu's roommate, arrived shortly afterwards and brushed and pinned my hair into a chignon. Carrie, who worked at the Mac counter at Macy's, showed up some time later to do my make-up—as a gift because we had become friends.

My hair and makeup were finally done, and I slipped on my dress, which now fit comfortably. Gideon came up to the apartment with her daughter, our flower girl, to take me to the church.

It was the most glorious fall day, even if it was a bit cold. The leaves were in full color, the air was crisp and dry, and the sun never stopped shining once all day. I couldn't help but feel that the sun was shining just for me, the way it had over the Parisian rooftops all those years back—that God was telling me He was pleased with me, that He was pleased with the wedding, and that He would give me sun, not just for my entrance, but for the whole day. My heart sung with praise and thanks.

Matthieu and I had been busy these last months. We had made time for dates; we had had intimate conversations about intertwining our lives. I felt such a mix of joy and rawness in that in-between stage where we were marching inexorably towards union, but were not yet there. *God please don't let me die before I get married. Don't let Matthieu die. Just let us get married, and then you can do what you want.*

Now, the day had arrived. I was terrified Matthieu would see me as I ran across the campus towards the church, but I only saw his mother who assured me he was nowhere nearby. The bridesmaids congregated with me in the red-carpeted basement when we heard the loud salsa music cueing Matthieu's entrance at the front of the church, the music which would accompany the entrance of his best men down the aisle. The fast, happy beat reverberated throughout the church.

Then Gloria whisked my bridesmaids upstairs, and their entrance song came on to usher them in. They were perfectly timed to reach the altar at an even pace, the last one arriving right as the song was ending. Then there was the expectant silence.

My father had come down to the basement where I was sitting alone. "Are you ready?" he asked affectionately.

"Yes." I smiled nervously at him. We walked up the stairs to stand outside the great wooden doors and heard the muted strains of music coming from inside. I watched the scene unfold in my mind.

Christianne and Sonja danced down the aisle and around the circular altar, each one half of a whole. The flower girl timidly dropped white rose petals as she went down the aisle, and the dancers turned back to escort her to where she lay petals at Matthieu's feet. From behind the young girl, the dancers curtsied to the floor, wood nymphs preparing the way for the bride.

The music began to swell with passion, and my flower girl ran to the safety of her father's arms on the side. "Are you okay?" my father asked, as he patted my arm on his. I was too nervous to look at him or to answer. I nodded.

The music soared louder as the dancers ran to the back of the church, their arms stretched, in front and in back, and just as the music rose to a pitch, they leapt to the right side and to the left to herald my entrance as the tall heavy doors swung outwards.

Suddenly, the church was bathed in sunlight and you could barely see our figures in the doorway. I had been given my sun. Escorted by warmth and rays of light, I felt like it was not only my father who was giving me away, but my Heavenly Father as well.

In a loud voice, the minister said, "All rise." The guests stood up with thundering applause as my father walked me down the aisle and handed me off to my husband-to-be.

As Jesus was coming up out of the water, he saw heaven being torn open and the Spirit descending on him like a dove. And a voice came from heaven: "You are my son, whom I love; with you I am well pleased." At once the Spirit sent him out into the desert and he was in the desert forty days, being tempted by Satan. He was with the wild animals, and the angels attended him." Mark 1

14

EAST AFRICA

I was finally married and so happy to come back to the same home each evening. But married life had no time to settle into boring routine before we were swept up again. I had gone through that spiritual desert of refinement after baptism, and had I given the matter any conscious thought, I would have assumed that was enough. I had done my time and was living out the rest of my life in peace and harmony. So I was wholly unprepared to be tossed into yet another desert after getting married; and this time it was an actual, physical desert, located in the Horn of Africa.

We started out on the lower East Side of Manhattan below Houston Street in a two-bedroom apartment. The neighborhood was diverse; we went to bed to the sound of salsa and ordered takeout meals of crispy, seasoned chicken, plantains, and rice and beans. This was a period of peace for me where I was happy and flourishing spiritually. I was learning a lot about gentleness from Matthieu and was starting to treat people with a spirit of grace, instead of bashing them over the head with my legalistic bat of righteousness.

I've since come to question the idea that just because I'm in a period of peace and harmony it means I'm doing well spiritually. I've started to think that it's rather a period of rest granted me—a respite before I'm plunged into battle again. I expected that life was going to be perfect now that I was married to the man I loved and our ministry was growing. All our strivings seemed to bear the stamp of approval from God. But Nirvana was not to be had, and my attempts to reach it were thwarted, much to my very great frustration.

We had only been married two months when we got the call to go to Africa. The message went something like this: "Hi Matthieu, this is Katie. Now don't freak out, but Malinda gave us your names as a recommendation to replace a couple on our team in Africa because we need someone who speaks French. Why don't you and your wife take some time to consider the idea and then give us a call back so we can talk more about it?" The call came from the charity associated with our church that organized projects worldwide to help the poor.

When Matthieu listened to the message, he was in the Atlanta Hewlett Packard lab, six stories underground. The entire room as far as he could see was filled with aisles and aisles of large servers, and he only emerged into the fresh air and fading sunlight when the workday was finished. He had been traveling a lot and thinking, despondently, "What am I doing here, so far away from my wife?"

But this call was a gateway to promised change, and his first thoughts were exultant. "Finally. Real life begins." I was no less enthusiastic about leaving everything and moving to Africa. We wasted no time in meeting the couple that headed the organization, and the only question we had for them was, "When do we get to go?" We left in April 2001 with a full five months of marital experience in our possession.

Our training was to take place in Hargeisa, Somaliland for two months with the remainder of our time spent in Djibouti. We had some vague ideas about the country, linking Somalia to pirates and its dangerous capital city of Mogadishu, but we were told that Hargeisa was peaceful. What we didn't know, and were corrected immediately upon making the gaffe, was that Somaliland was actually a different country than Somalia. They had split following the civil war with Mogadishu in the South, and though it was unrecognized by the UN, Somaliland had managed to remain a peaceful country ever since 1989.

We had a few months to prepare. I quit my new job with JP Morgan while my husband asked for a sabbatical from his. I went to the outlet stores in New Jersey, trying to find outfits that were modest and could be worn in hot weather. I was impatient through the preparatory period and couldn't wait to be on our way. I relished the fact that I would finally get to travel with someone else instead of going alone and found it reassuring that the someone was Matthieu.

We first flew to Addis Ababa in Ethiopia, stopping only in Rome to refuel. I stepped out of the plane onto the rolling staircase platform and stretched my limbs, breathing in the night air that smelled of jet fuel and listening to the people down below yelling at each other in Italian.

We were only in Addis for a few hours, and if I thought that airport was tiny, I no longer thought so when we landed in Hargeisa. The steps were let down from the medium-sized aircraft, and we climbed down onto the dirt runway, squinting in the bright sunlight and feeling the dry air blow on our faces. In front of us was a small, white, concrete building with people bustling around it.

Christian, a member of the team, met us there and introduced us to the driver, Abdi Hakim, before going over to get our entry papers sorted out. The driver yelled at some of the men to grab our bags and carry them to the truck, and they quickly obeyed. Everyone was staring at us curiously.

The truck bumped and jolted over the potholes on the road as we drove at breakneck speed, our driver frequently swerving to the side of the road to find a smoother surface. The scenery whipped by, blending the browns and yellows of the trees and sand with the simple white buildings, marred by the bombing and shelling from over a decade earlier. There was some green, but the main touches of color I saw were the pastel pink, blue, and yellow plastic bags that the desert wind swept into the spiny tree branches where they remained in colorful knots. The "Hargeisa Flower," it was called.

We arrived at the door to our yellow compound, and the driver got out and banged on the gate for the guards to let us in. Mike, Petrina, and Malinda immediately came out with big smiles to greet us, followed by the staff that stood about shyly. Most of them didn't speak English. The women were wearing long cotton shift dresses that they tucked into their nylon lace slips on one side to keep the dress from trailing on the ground. Their heads were covered, some casually with pretty colored cloth and others wrapped tightly in beige or navy polyester, which revealed only their cheeks and forehead.

The compound walls enclosed a yard leading to the open porch with grass and a small number of trees. The area behind the house was lusher. The two buildings there served as an office and a bedroom for Christian. Above the small patch of grass and purple plants, a clothesline stretched across cement posts.

The interior of the compound was simple. The floors were made of tile and linoleum, and there was rattan matting on the floor with small cushioned couches that served as a living area. The sturdy table was as roughly hewn as the beds. We wheeled our suitcases into the room and looked at the four wooden posts on the corners of the bed that held the canopy of mosquito netting. We unpacked our clothes and put them on the unfinished wooden shelves.

Mike and Petrina were the lead couple on the team and had already been there for a year, along with Malinda and Christian. Petrina proposed that we women take a drive after we had had some time to unpack. An hour later, we were dropped off in an uninhabited part of the desert along the barren road where we could walk on the firm sand. We found a place to sit at the base of a small hill. There was no one else in sight.

"Look around you," she said. "I wanted to come here because I thought we could take a moment to appreciate how beautiful it is before we all get caught up in routine." I breathed in the clean, dry air and looked at the late afternoon sun above the hillside as I let the cool sand slip through my fingers. As far as I could see, there were small sand dunes sporting patches of tenacious plants, and there were two larger hills in the distance.

Looking back at my faith during that year in Africa, I can see that it was like those desert shrubs I saw on the hillside—barely watered, but with tough enough roots to keep the shrub from tumbling away. There was little rainfall that year, and my soul was not nourished in any way that I could actually see. As I stumbled from one bewildering adventure to another, I often felt disconnected from God. It seemed only my roots kept me from drifting away.

Our life in Hargeisa was so all-consuming we barely gave thought to our mission in Djibouti. This neighboring country shared the same race, clans, language, and religion as the Somali people, and we learned that this was an unusual thing to find in one country in Africa, much less two. We would be leaning on the team in Somaliland for support, and our two-month training period to acclimate was vital.

The orphanage was one place where we focused our attention, and it was not far from our compound. We walked along the sandy gravel on the side of the road, clothed in the local dress, our heads veiled in colorful cloth. As soon as we arrived, hordes of children crowded around us, grinning up at us and trying to draw our attention. It was hard to content ourselves with just giving them the attention they craved and ignoring the deplorable state in which they lived.

In the morning, about four toddlers sat on potties as a way of mass potty training. In the small dim room that served as a nursery, one or two women bustled around the half dozen cribs, an infant in every cot. Because there was so much to do, the bottles were sometimes simply propped up next to the babies. If they were not strong enough to drink, there was no guarantee they would get all the milk they needed.

The nursery became my favorite destination because I felt like I could do something there. When the older children crowded around me, I kept a smile plastered on my face and held light conversation, mixing simple English and sign language. With the older kids, I left dissatisfied because it didn't seem I was making a difference with them. So what if I cut a few nails or inexpertly braided a few heads of hair? Were they any better off than they were before? At the time, I didn't think so.

But in the nursery, I came alive. I went in and tentatively picked the babies up, cooing at them, caressing them, and feeding them with a medicine dropper if they were too weak to suck on the bottle. I brought them out into the sun, changed their soaked diapers, cleaned their small bodies from diarrhea, and rocked and sang to them. I tried to swallow my First World opinions and help the orphanage workers without judgment. When I saw how neglected the babies seemed, I was not always successful in curbing the internal superiority. But I was pleased to see concrete improvements through my ministrations with babies like Khadra, who started to fatten up with regular attention.

The first time we went to the Maternity Hospital, that was under construction with plans to open later that year, I met its formidable owner, Edna Adan. She managed to give the impression of being supremely in charge of everything, and at the same time, having all the time in the world for us. She didn't waste her words on anything benign; everything she said was educative or inspiring or entertaining or persuasive. I felt like I should carry a notebook when I was with her; she was the most remarkable woman I had ever met.

Over the months, she let little stories fall as if they had no more significance than taking afternoon tea. Stories like how a seriously wounded young man was brought into her hospital, followed by the soldiers who wanted to kill him. The soldiers pointed their shotguns at him and told her to get out of the way so they could shoot him, but she yelled at them until they were too abashed to carry out the execution.

"Besides, he's nearly dead anyway," she said. "Look at him." She lifted the compress off his wound, letting his blood spurt everywhere. "Pretend to be dead," she muttered under her breath, standing over her patient. Her showdown resulted in his captors' departure without meeting their objective, and she and the young man became friends.

She had been inspired to her calling by her father, a doctor and prominent figure in Hargeisa in his day. She studied nursing and midwifery in Djibouti and then in England. As a young woman, she married the man who would later become the Prime Minister of Somalia. "I politely put up with the visits of General Siad Barre," she said. "I clucked quietly to myself when he got shoe polish on my couch and scattered cigarette ashes on my rug. I shouldn't have been surprised when he staged a coup, arrested my husband, and had me put under house arrest."

"Ah," she sighed. "I was under house arrest for months. If it weren't for my friendship with a Somali woman who didn't fear the local government, I would have had no drinking water or any other basic necessities." She shook her head. "No one else dared bring me anything."

Edna continued her story matter-of-factly. "When Somaliland freed itself from its oppressors in the south, the people of Somaliland elected a president, and it was my former husband, the one who had been the prime minister before the coup. We had divorced by then," she added.

"I decided to do something to help my country, and I approached my ex-husband to ask for a plot of land where I could build a maternity hospital. He kept putting me off, but I wouldn't let it go. Finally, because I was so persistent, he gave me a small plot of land in the slums. It was meant to be an insult."

"It was the site of a former graveyard," she went on indignantly, "not far from the mass graves where the army tied men, women, and children together and had them stand in front of the hole that held hundreds of dead bodies. Then they shot them until the people all fell dead into it. And *this* was where I was meant to build my hospital."

But Edna was an unstoppable force. "What better place to have a maternity hospital where we usher in new life than a place that was once laden with death? Plus," she reasoned, "if it's in the slums, we'll really be reaching the people who need it most."

Before Edna's hospital was built, Somaliland had one of the highest infant-mother mortality rates. One of the contributing problems was that most women were still being circumcised, although Edna was working hard to eliminate the practice through education campaigns.

"So you can imagine a woman giving birth in the bush," she said, "standing up and holding on to a low branch as she pushes her child out, and the inevitable tearing and bleeding that follows. But now these people have hope of getting medical attention," she continued with satisfaction. "And they often leave the bush and come into the city just to give birth here."

In those first two months, I taught the nursing students English. I tried to introduce them to what was happening around the world, and not just grammar. Once I brought my favorite movie, *Braveheart*, for them to see. I thought this story of resilience and courage was perfect for a group of young people who were living in rather desperate living situations and fighting hard to surmount the challenges. Some of my students had never seen a movie or television show before, and they watched with wide eyes, completely swept up in the story. These young women were living in a time warp, carved out by poverty.

While I was helping the students achieve a basic level of English, my husband spent time setting up the computers that were donated to the hospital. Together, we hoped they would one day be able to search the Web easily to find information that would assist them in their nursing. Years later, I learned from Edna that it was, indeed, the case. Many of my former students went on to train other nurses and midwives, and still others enrolled in the new universities in Somaliland. But truthfully, in a third world country, you can leave off the fancy diplomas—any experience is better than none, and many of those students acquired great expertise in trial-by-fire once the hospital opened.

Sometimes we asked our driver to take us deep into the desert, so we could go running at the close of day when it was cool. Our whole team went, and we women feared being unveiled in front of the nomads less than we did in town. Abdi Hakim followed us slowly along the road with the car, never once taking his eye off us, and we felt protected under his constant presence and vigilance. There I saw caravans of camels walking by. They were impressive in their size and stateliness, and their feet were surprisingly soft and squishy in the sand.

We were fortunate to have a good cook, so we could focus our efforts on those in need rather than picking pebbles out of grains of rice. But our cook had Fridays off, so it was up to us to head to the market and see what sort of things we could find to cook up ourselves.

The market was simple with a few makeshift tents and people selling various goods and services. One woman sewed our fabric into the cotton shifts we wore, pedaling the black iron sewing machine to get a line of stitching. Several stalls had freshly slaughtered goat, and the carcass was covered with buzzing flies. We chose our portion of meat, and the vendor hacked at the piece of flesh until he had separated it; then he wiped the cleaver on the top of the tent where more flies gathered.

Other stalls were even simpler—women sitting on a blanket shielded from the sun by a small piece of tarp. They were selling an array of things, like a few tomatoes, a half cabbage, some small onions, a chili pepper, and a bowl of potatoes. Few of them were wealthy enough to have a large stash, and we tried to buy from everyone as equally as we could.

I developed a taste for cold Coca-Cola and Fanta, which I bought at the small concrete corner store. The cold bubbly sweetness was never more appreciated than when living in the hot desert climate of East Africa.

Eggs were difficult to find as you could never be sure which store or market would have any. This resulted in my only fight with Petrina.

"But I used all my eggs for the fried rice for the *entire* team. Surely you can spare *two* of your eggs for us," I demanded hotly.

"No. I bought these especially for Mike," Petrina answered, whose husband loved omelets. Everyone teased us both, and it broke through our momentary tension until we were both laughing too.

We were befriended by some of our Somali neighbors, and they introduced us to camel's milk, which was supposed to have all sorts of health benefits. But it was such a salty, horrifying thing to drink I couldn't bear to take more than a sip. I much preferred the home-cooked, stone-ground coffee ritual that our Ethiopian cook treated us to.

The neighbors also invited us to share in their ritual of perfuming. Our hair was heavily laced with cologne, and we stood over a smoking clay pot with our long cotton dresses while delightfully scented incense permeated our bodies and the fabric of our dresses. A later attempt to replicate the ritual back in New York resulted in a singularly embarrassing experience as I cleared a wide berth around me in the subway car.

The staff at the hospital made spiced samosas for us—fried dough, stuffed with flavored ground goat meat, which we ate along with our hot, sweet chai tea. At night, we gathered around the small television to watch an eclectic stash of DVDs. On a few evenings, we women applied a green facemask made of a local plant called Qasil, mixed with water to form a thick paste. It was the local ritual for beautiful skin, and it left ours soft and glowing.

The cleaners swept a wet rag over the tile floor every day to clean the persistent accumulation of sand, and negotiated among themselves who was going to make the heavily sugared Somali tea that was for their own consumption. They took our laundry and washed it in shallow buckets, pounding the clothes clean and hanging them to dry.

We asked the guards to refrain from chewing khat—leaves you could chew to get a buzz, and which became dangerous with long-term use. But apart from chewing, they didn't have a whole lot to do other than sit there, and it was a challenge for them to resist this small pleasure.

We weren't in much danger in our compound, and if we had been, there was little they could do about it without weapons. One night, an irate person with a grudge set off a bomb in our neighbor's compound, and it shook the foundations of our own. Fortunately, no one was hurt from the incident, although everyone on our team ran out to the guard to see what had happened. I slept soundly through the whole thing.

We could not have done without a driver as there was no insurance in Somaliland. If someone got hurt, or a car got totaled, the elders of the two clans got together and decided the proper recompense. If you didn't belong to a clan, you had no one to take your side.

Not knowing what clan they belonged to hurt some of the orphans the most. In Muslim culture, and especially in Somaliland, orphans were nearly as likely as anyone else to succeed if they could survive the poor sanitary conditions of the orphanage. But some orphans were left at the gate with no trace of their heritage, and those unnamed orphans had little hope.

Dowood was one such orphan who didn't know to which clan he belonged. As if his lack of identity was not enough, the orphanage director lost his mind during the civil war and started shooting randomly at the orphans, hitting Dowood in the leg when he was just two years old. Dowood desperately felt his perceived lack of worth and had already tried to commit suicide at least once by the time I met him at the age of twelve.

Our electricity went on every day from eight to eleven at night, and any other electricity we needed we got through a generator. The lights were so dim when we finally did have electricity I could barely read. All our food had to be eaten daily because the refrigerator wasn't on long enough to keep things cold. The water was not drinkable, so we boiled it or drank bottled water.

When we took a shower, it was frigid (the desert is not hot in the mornings, only in the afternoons), and we jumped in, squealing and hyperventilating. Our hygienic standards reached a new low. "Oh, I washed my hair four days ago. I can go another day."

However, there was a simplistic joy in crawling into the rough-hewn beds, covered with netting, the fresh night air pouring in through the open windows, the guard sitting in the compound making quiet movements as he settled down for the night. There was simple pleasure in rubbing oneself off vigorously after a freezing cold shower and dressing in a clean cotton shift before sitting down with a steaming cup of tea.

There was this feeling of wonder, climbing up the ladder to the flat roof of the compound and sitting there, staring at a sky full of stars like you've never seen—a view somewhat spoiled when they installed a neon light at a gas station a few roads over. Still, if you lay down, you couldn't see the light—just the blackness of the night, the plethora of stars showering the night sky with white glitter, and the frequent shooting stars cutting silently across the expanse.

At sunrise came the call to prayer over the loudspeakers. That set off the sound of a rooster crowing in the kitchen, if that's what our cook had decided we would be eating for lunch.

I planted myself in this country, the dry air brushing my face and bracing my limbs as I waited to see what would come. I was getting my bearings, numbly pushing roots into the desert soil in search of something stronger to attach myself to—in search of my water source. How little I imagined that these two months were a period of respite. And I was going to need it.

Though the fig tree does not bud and there are no grapes on the vines, though the olive crop fails and the fields produce no food, though there are no sheep in the pen and no cattle in the stalls, yet I will rejoice in the Lord, I will be joyful in God my Savior. Habakkuk 3

15

THE DESERT

The border between Somaliland and Djibouti was closed again when it was time for us to move there. This was nothing new as there were frequent border disputes between the neighboring countries, but it turned what would have been a quick forty-five minute plane trip into an all-day affair.

I tentatively followed Matthieu into the Daallo Airlines plane that looked like it was from the 1950s with a bulbous cockpit and fat wings. Some of the seats had been ripped out of their casings, leaving the bolts exposed on the floor. We searched for two seats together that still had the seat belts attached. I was surprised to notice that the two pilots were white, although I didn't recognize the language they spoke. I soon learned that these men were Russian, a necessity for the Daallo planes, which had been imported from Russia and had controls only legible to those who spoke the language.

We flew for an hour and a half in the opposite direction of Djibouti to a city called Bosaso, in the region of Puntland on the coast. I looked out the window as the plane circled down for the landing and noticed that the runway was close to the edge of the ocean. There was nothing in sight but sand, a tiny concrete building with a chain-link fence, and a few soldiers.

Our plane touched down on the sandy tarmac, and we stepped out into the dry heat. "I'd like to find a bathroom," I said, as we stood around waiting. Christian had accompanied us on this trip since he had contacts in the government, and he offered to ask one of the soldiers.

"It's way over there," he said when he returned, pointing to the concrete hut. "But be quick about it. The plane won't wait for you, and we need to be certain that we get a seat for the next leg because it's first-come, first-serve."

"What?" I said. "But our luggage is on the plane, and we have a ticket."

"That does not matter one bit," he replied.

Matthieu walked with me across the open, vulnerable expanse towards the soldiers. It was far, and the plane looked small when we looked back. Upon inquiry, the unsmiling soldiers pointed to a tiny wooden outhouse with their automatic weapons. It had no roof, and there was not even a hole in the style of a Turkish toilet. It was just a cement mound with sloped sides to let the urine trickle down outside the walls. I squatted down anyway, knowing I had a near three-hour plane ride with no toilet ahead of me.

We returned to the group congregated beside the plane. Suddenly, there was a sound of automatic weapons firing, and everyone around me ducked under the wings. The sound didn't seem close, so I stayed where I was, but Christian pulled us back towards the protection of the plane.

When we landed in Djibouti and stepped on to the tarmac, I experienced a blistering wave of heat like I'd never felt, not even living in Taiwan or traveling further south in Asia. It was a pounding heat with heavy, humid air that took your breath away. We walked over to the stand where we got our temporary papers until we could replace them at the consulate. Then we climbed into a taxi with our luggage and headed to the apartment.

The former team, which consisted of just one couple and the occasional help of Christian, had already started the registration process over six months earlier to be a government-recognized charity. The registration was still not complete, and we were not allowed to do anything until it was if we wanted to remain in good graces with the government.

Christian was staying in a hotel, and he left us at the furnished apartment to check in and relax for a few hours. I looked around our new home in dismay at the dirt and sundry items, which had been hastily strewn about by the previous couple, who had every intention of returning, but who—for personal reasons—was unable to renew their contract. Matthieu, recognizing the frozen look on my face, started filling buckets with water and soap, and shoving the clothes and non-valuables lying on the floor into a garbage bag.

When we had settled in and bleached the whole apartment, removing the dead cockroaches and garbage, Christian came to take us around to visit. At first glance, the city was depressing. It was First World gone awry—rows and rows of buildings that had a European feel to them, but which were decaying in the poverty and heat. Some people walked by, brisk and business-like; others sat dejectedly on the steps. There were a few cafés and restaurants with people at the outdoor tables, but they were uninviting in the dirt and heat.

I kept thinking, *this is where we'll be for almost a year. This is the place I've come to serve and love.* But I couldn't match my spirits to my determination in the soul-sucking heat, decrepit buildings, and poverty.

"I'm going to take you to a nice café," Christian said, and brought us down a few more streets before entering an obscure doorway that had an elevator just inside. He punched number four, and we went up.

When we stepped off the elevator, there was a glass door, which opened into a cheerful, airy café where a welcoming blast of air conditioning met us. Half the walls were bay windows, which overlooked the port with massive ships that were loading or dropping off cargo. For the first time since we arrived, Djibouti looked beautiful. From this vantage point in the cool café, we were above the filth and saw just the blue skies and blue water of the ocean. I ordered a Perrier with mint syrup.

As the cool, dry air whisked the humidity away from my skin, and the icy mint drink further refreshed me, my spirits began to rise. We could do this. We were going to be okay.

Christian wasted no time in presenting our consultant, Ahmed, who was the liaison for the government and charitable contacts. We spent a lot of time with him, even after Christian returned to Hargeisa, because we didn't know anyone else. He was equally pleased with the arrangement because it ensured he would be earning money and having his expenses paid on a regular basis. We went out to dinner together, and he brought us to meetings to discuss potential projects.

The orphanage was in a much better state than the one in Hargeisa. The orphans wore uniforms, slept in dorms, and had some schooling, rather than wearing scraps of clothing and playing in the dirt. There was running water, swings, a library, and even workshops where they could learn artisan trades. We offered to teach English and computers or serve in whatever way we could, despite the fact that everything already seemed to be running smoothly. We also met the university director with whom we discussed potential teaching positions. He was delighted to learn that we would do this for free.

However, because of the bureaucracy, so much time was spent doing nothing as the weeks passed. We woke up in our tiny one-bedroom apartment in the city center with the air conditioning running blessedly at full blast. We took a shower and got ready to go out into the scorching wet heat, sometimes for no other reason than for form's sake; we couldn't stay in the apartment all day, every day. We walked down the balcony that ran along the apartments, its rail strung with clothing lines attached to the balcony on the other side. By the time we got to the staircase, sweat was already dripping freely down our bodies.

On our self-enforced promenades, we went to the main grocery store in the center of town. This was a pleasure after living in Hargeisa because we could find items like good cheese, chocolate, coffee, and other culinary treasures. As a former French colony, Djibouti retained much French influence, particularly when it came to cuisine. For the first two shopping trips, we tried to buy extra food for the crowd of people begging outside, but we quickly stopped that practice when we saw that, rather than helping, we were starting a riot.

Sometimes at night, particularly when we were with Ahmed, we headed over to the outdoor restaurant on the dock to eat fish. When the sun went down, there was a slight breeze that moved the languid heat enough to make it bearable near the water. We tried to make friends with the people Ahmed and Christian knew, but they were all busy and not eager to add to their circle of acquaintances. The few times I tried to set something up, it always came to nothing, and Matthieu and I found ourselves alone most of the time.

When Christian came back from Hargeisa to visit us, we went jogging together during the "cool" part of the day, running along the busy streets and the wharf as the sailors looked at us curiously. We went to a movie—an outdoor showing of *Cast Away* with Tom Hanks, and for once I forgot the heat, the fact that the movie was in French, the people seated all around me. I forgot everything else and was lost in a story in which the plight of the main character seemed so pertinent to my own. We were privileged; I was cognizant of the fact. But we were isolated, out of place, and lonely—this was poverty of a different sort.

Our favorite café remained the first one we had gone to on the fourth floor, and we went almost every day. I became friendly with the woman who worked there, and we kept up a cheerful banter whenever we saw each other. Once when I complimented her on the flimsy red scarf she used to tie around her head, which was so pretty against her light brown skin, she unwound it and gave it to me on the spot, ignoring my protests.

She invited us to her home, begged us to come, promising to accompany us there on the bus and then bring us back to the bus stop so we could get home. Matthieu and I went, and as I left the city center and traveled further out into the desert, I saw the shack-like houses with tin corrugated roofs, so unlike the nomads' tents that were in Somaliland. I couldn't fathom how they could bear the heat, enclosed in there with the sun beating on the metal roof.

When we finally arrived at her modest, open-air house, I sat down uncomfortably in the sweltering heat, finding my place on the floor where she had indicated. She sat down across from us, lit a fire under the bong that was in the middle of our circle, and took off her bra inside her dress, pulling it out through her short sleeve. I was shocked by her welcome and hoped that my husband hadn't noticed the bra.

She offered us a cold drink, which we accepted, but otherwise seemed quite content to smoke and make sparse conversation, not minding that we had refused her invitation to take a hit. We left as soon as we politely could, and I never again felt comfortable around her after that visit. When she asked me to give her some money to replace the mouthpiece to her bong, I told her no. That wasn't how I wanted to donate money.

Everything we did was slow and heavy because of the blanket of hot, oppressive humidity. When we didn't feel obligated to go out we stayed safely at home in our air-conditioned apartment. We didn't have a television or radio, so we dug into the stash of English books left behind by the previous couple. I started reading *The Poisonwood Bible*, chuckling often at the bumbling description of the missionary, and my laughter piqued Matthieu's curiosity. I ended up reading the book out loud to him. The story was strangely apropos, and reading the irony and humor that slowly gave way to tragedy brought us closer. We also made a set of cards out of cardboard so we could play games in the evenings. Though we were never lacking in conversation, I once laid my hands flat on the table and looked across at him, my eyes brimming with tears. "I'm so lonely," I said.

"Me too," he answered solemnly.

Since the border was closed between Somaliland and Djibouti, we couldn't call the team in Hargeisa and ended up leaning on the church in Nairobi for moral and spiritual support. An American couple led the church there, and they started checking in with us on a regular basis.

We sent e-mails from the Internet café with its slow, dial-up connection, and we had to pay careful attention to everything we wrote. Any talk of Christianity could jeopardize our work there.

A few people, whose opinion we trusted, encouraged us to move into a rented house on the beach. Since our only experience in Africa so far had consisted of living in an NGO (Non-Governmental Organization) compound with a guard, it seemed like the right thing to do. We were told that in Africa, presence and image was everything, and if we wanted to be taken seriously as an NGO, we needed to put up a good front. With the goal of setting the stage for future workers to come over and have a proper presence in the country, we thought we were making a good decision at the time; so did our headquarters.

However, if we found it lonely cooped up in our apartment, we were further isolated in the house. It was more of a walk to get to the city center, so we were less inspired to go. We didn't want to pay to air condition the entire empty house, so we ended up spending most of the time in our bedroom. Without realizing it, we were slowly drawing ourselves inward as time went on.

A chain link fence marked the edge of the property, which overlooked the ocean and bordered a heavily crowded public beach. As foreigners, we wouldn't be welcome to swim in the ocean (even if we weren't already deterred by the fact that it was dirty and crowded), so we could only look out at them from our position of "privilege," feeling strangely left out.

I was no longer inspired to cook because that meant being swelteringly hot. We couldn't get cold water from the faucets to refresh ourselves, and with its high salt content, you couldn't boil it for drinking water or tea. When I washed our clothes in the bathtub and wrung them out to hang on the clotheslines outside, that small effort sent me straight to the shower. I swept the corridor and left a clean floor sprinkled with trails of salty droplets as sweat dripped off my nose.

Just as we were reaching our breaking point of boredom and isolation, we got the news that our papers had been approved. We were a legally recognized charity in Djibouti, and we could begin work there without delay. This renewed our enthusiasm for our mission. We would start teaching at the orphanage and university, as promised, and then see what we could do from there. As this news came at a time when we were just beginning to make friends with some Ethiopians who were living there for work, we saw everything coming together as a divine sign of hope—the parting of the Red Sea, a dove carrying an olive branch.

One or two days into our preparation, Matthieu was in the office listening to the radio, and I was sitting on the bed reading. Suddenly he burst into the bedroom, his face registering shock.

"Something happened in New York," he said. "A plane flew into the Twin Towers."

"What?" I felt the blood drain from my face. "What happened?" Since he couldn't answer me, we went back into the office to try and catch more of the story but were interrupted by a phone call from Ahmed. He had heard the news and was coming to pick us up and take us to a café where we could watch CNN.

We watched the news footage from the dark café, feeling numb and helpless, as our drinks sat untouched on the table. The terrible scene unfolded in a place so familiar to us, while we ourselves were far away. It wasn't a plane—it was a terrorist attack on our country. It was not an accident, it was unspeakable horror.

That night we spent hours on the phone, regardless of the cost, trying to reach all the people we knew. Though the lines were often clogged, what little news we had brought relief. Petrina, our team-member in Hargeisa, told us that her brother had changed jobs a week before the attack. He had been working in the top floor of the First Tower. As we processed all the news, good and bad, somewhere on the periphery of our consciousness was the awareness that we were living in a Muslim country.

The local people expressed only grief, shock, and condemnation over the terrorist act. However, in Somaliland, there had been a few less-peaceful incidents. A young boy commanded me with glowering eyes to put my veil back on because I was being vulgar by letting it slip backwards off my head in the heat. A pick-up truck zoomed in front of us as we were walking in the desert, and a young man called out to us from the back. "Go home—we don't want you here." A car pulled up sharply against me on the side of the road and knocked the bag of groceries out of my hand. Naive, and impervious to danger, I went up to the car window, and looked him in the eyes, asking him, "Why?" — one of the few words I knew in Somali. Finally, a police officer shook off his lethargy, spat out his khat, and came running over to yell at them.

There were the subtle threats and also the more serious element of danger that happened months prior to our stay, which threatened our peace. A British national, working outside of Hargeisa, had been sitting inside her car with the window open when a man came up with a large knife and stabbed her in the back. The driver ran after the man instead of trying to get help for her, and she bled to death before help could arrive.

We knew what risks were involved, but the danger and prejudice we experienced were more the exception than the norm. In Djibouti, we were even more removed from the threat of violence as there were more Europeans, and women were not expected to wear veils. None of the danger I braced myself for as I moved to Africa could have prepared me for the war that would occur in the comfortable, modern city that contained my friends and home back in New York.

Matthieu and I were numb; we were spiritually hollowed out. After our government approval, the only thing that made sense was to keep moving forward and set up the projects. A few days later, our headquarters decided to evacuate us along with the Hargeisa team, following the example of the other international NGOs in Somaliland. I tried to protest—we were fine, we couldn't leave now just when things were starting. But the orders had come in, and we began to spread the word that we were leaving.

Our consultant, the institutions we had promised to help, and our contacts in the American consulate were shocked that we were leaving to go to the nebulous safety of Nairobi (despite the fact that there was a known Al-Qaida camp in the outskirts of Djibouti proper). We faced the decision squarely—with embarrassment, but not a little relief. Our headquarters rightly wanted the whole East African team together, and so we would go.

It is also possible that the concerned people in our headquarters heard in our voices the loneliness, grief, and desperation of being thrown in the desert for so long with little local support. Within a week's time, we found ourselves at the airport, smiling wryly at the security officer's bumbling attempts to ensure there were no bombs in our luggage for the first time in his career.

"Are you sure there's no bomb in there? It's just a camera, you say? Because, you know, if it's a bomb, it's not me up there in that airplane. You're the one who will go down."

Then we were on a plane bound for Kenya, leaving behind the

discouragement that characterized our three months in Djibouti. We had a house, but had no one to live in it; we had made promises, but had no time to fulfill them. In Djibouti, nothing was planted and nothing had grown.

And the soil of our hearts had become so arid, cracked, and dry in the drought, we were no longer aware of our thirst.

They go from strength to strength, till each appears before God in Zion.
Psalm 84

16

A TEMPERATE OASIS

We arrived when Nairobi was in a profusion of color. It was fall, so the weather was warm and dry, the foliage lush and in full bloom; the soil was so rich, even the houseplants reached gargantuan proportions. I passed an aloe plant that was nearly twice my height and twice my width.

Someone from the church met Matthieu and me at the airport, and they brought us, and all our possessions, to a family living in the outskirts with whom we would be staying. Their names were Beatrice and Aggrey, and their daughter, Alison, spoke only a mixture of Swahili and their own tribal language. The house was cheerful and modern with a well-kept front lawn and American-style furnishings that lent immediate feelings of home. The guest bedroom was located on the ground floor off the living room, and it had its own private bathroom. The rest of the family had their bedrooms upstairs.

Their maid came from Uganda. She was engaged to someone back home and planned on finishing her year with the family before rejoining him for the wedding. She simply couldn't afford to turn down a steady paycheck until she absolutely had to. She brought us dinner upstairs in the family room every evening, and we ate it while watching the news or a Spanish soap opera with English subtitles.

The standard fare consisted of ugali (*oo-gah-lee*), sukuma wiki (*soo-koo-ma week-ee*) and gizzards. Ugali was a white corn porridge, pressed into a cake and sliced into pieces like bread. We broke off chunks of the cake and molded them into a spoon to scoop up the meat and vegetables. Sukuma wiki meant, "push the week," and was a mixture of collard greens and kale in a flavored tomato sauce. This was the cheap dish people made when money was tight until the next paycheck came in and they could afford to buy meat again. This was how one "pushed the week."

After a few days, we started to wonder when we would need to find someplace to live; after all, we couldn't expect to inconvenience these nice people forever. That's when Beatrice and Aggrey made it clear they expected us to continue staying with them as long as we were in Nairobi. They did ask us to contribute towards the living expenses, which we did gladly, but otherwise treated us like part of the family and didn't ask for rent. We were touched, and from them learned what it truly meant to be hospitable.

As we ate dinner and watched the news, we learned about the corruption that often occurred, even at the governmental level. Beatrice told me how, a few years earlier, a government official had agreed to split the difference in gain with a corrupt businessman who sold chalk to the city, instead of chlorine, to purify the water. As a result of his greed, thousands died from cholera and typhoid.

Our own water supply was clean, although we still drank it boiled, and it was only available on a limited basis. The city brought water to our suburb just two and a half days out of the week, and that's when we could get it directly from the faucet. The first thing the maid did on Mondays was to fill the huge canteens in the garden with water to last us the rest of the week. I usually washed our clothes in those first two days, plunging the items in cold soapy water outside and hanging them up to dry.

The sun was hot, but the air was fresh, and the whole garden buzzed with insects and life. The trees in the garden provided some shade, and Matthieu and I wrung the clothes out with our hands before shaking them and hanging them on the clothesline to dry. Overhead, birds called "kites," which resembled small eagles, circled the property in graceful sweeps. Our senses breathed in the colorful beauty and scented perfumes floating through the cool, pure air. This was a pleasurable change from Djibouti.

Because water was scarce, we were asked not to take a shower, even on the two days that water ran from the faucets. Instead, we hooked an electric water heater to the side of a large bucket of water. When it was scalding, we poured half into a baby bathtub and added cold water to make it bearable. Then, standing in the regular bathtub, we poured water over ourselves with a faded red plastic pot. We soaped and shampooed, then rinsed ourselves off again, using just the amount of water needed to get clean.

The first time we ventured into the city by public transportation, Mike and Petrina accompanied us. They had stayed in Beatrice and Aggrey's guest room when they visited the year before and knew the neighborhood. We walked past the gated properties to where the road turned and we could climb the hill to the busy street. Two young, white men in shirts and ties walked past us down the hill. I looked at them curiously, finding them just as out of place as we were. "They're Mormon," Petrina explained. "They usually do mission work for a year when they're just out of school."

The buses, called matatu (*mah-tah-too*), were usually little more than a private minivan. We paid the small fare and took the bus to the city center before walking to the YMCA where the church held its midweek service. There, on the restaurant terrace, Petrina spotted people she knew from church and brought us over to be introduced. The restaurant overlooked a swimming pool and a grassy, shaded area, and we rested our gaze on the vegetation. Before long, it was time for service to begin, and we headed down the path to a concrete building with tiny windows, hidden behind the swimming pool and trees. Inside, there were rows of chairs and a few microphones.

The singing was fantastic. It was so good to hear the same familiar songs from our church in New York, sung with such abandon, and to hear other songs sung energetically in Swahili. It was a relief to express our faith openly, to pray with other people, to hear a message preached, and to get hugs from people I hadn't met yet, but who most definitely felt like family. In that first service, I started to understand why we were pulled out of Djibouti. I understood how much we needed to be here.

This service started the rhythm of our days in Kenya. Since we were there for an unknown, and assumedly short, period of time, we got more involved in ministry work than humanitarian aid. We were given a set number of people to meet with weekly and counsel spiritually, and we met with a couple who did the same thing for us. Most of our meetings were held at the YMCA where we ordered a lunch of sausage or gizzards and french fries with a cold orange Fanta.

Spending our energy on developing friendships was a satisfying way to spend our days. We sat on the terrace and listened to the birds chirping in the trees below and watched people swimming in the outdoor pool, splashing with gleeful cries. We belonged in a way we never could have as a tourist.

Some days, instead of the YMCA, we went to the Sarit Center, which was a small shopping mall. We found a tiny café in the food court that had scones and strong, steaming black coffee; just one sip seemed to boost my mood for the entire day. Sometimes we went to the mall for no other purpose than to start our day with breakfast.

For shopping, we went to the markets that sold cheap or second hand clothing, shoes, and bags. There were also specialty markets, like the Maasai Market. Their crafts were beautifully beaded in bright colors, and I bought a key chain that I knew would always remind me of my stay there.

We spent some time visiting the country. When we drove to the Rift Valley, just a short distance from where we were staying, I spotted some of the Maasai tribe herding cattle. Then, out of the corner of my eye, I saw an enormous bird taking flight. I asked what it was, but neither Beatrice nor Aggrey had seen it. Later, I saw the same birds perched on enormous nests in the tree branches extending over the streets of Nairobi. We were driving too quickly for me to get a good look, but at least I was able to learn that they were marabou storks.

Finally, I was given my chance to see these birds up close. We were early for church one Sunday, and I went off alone to the back of the church where there was a soccer field and a small set of bleachers. As soon as I climbed onto the empty bench, I noticed that the field was filled with large birds with white heads and necks—my marabou storks. They wandered around nearby, eating whatever they could find in the grass, completely ignoring me. I tried to commit such a magnificent sight to memory. I was awestruck to be that close to such a foreign species of bird, and it made me feel like I was indeed far from home.

After a few weeks in Kenya, we went on a day safari. We climbed into the bus and drove through the bush, snapping pictures of the zebras and faded giraffes in the distance. We only had one glimpse of the lions, but they were too far away to see anything. When the tour guide stopped and told us it was safe to get off the bus and stretch our legs, I was frightened to be in the open and tried to stay as close to the bus as possible.

I was still taking antidepressants, even during our stay in Africa. Apart from that two-year period following my baptism, I was no longer able to function without my perception of reality darkening and becoming unbearable. Before moving to Africa, a new psychiatrist switched the antidepressant medication from Prozac to Celexa because the Prozac didn't seem to be working anymore. I had the medicine sent to me, a few months at a time, during my year overseas.

Celexa calmed my anxiety—a huge plus, given our living conditions—and mastered my depression. However, I didn't know this antidepressant was a known contributor to weight gain, nor would I have been able to do much about it. In that one year, I gained twenty-five pounds without significantly changing the amount of food I was eating. I really started to notice the change while living in Kenya and began buying more clothes at the market to cover up my expanding figure. I didn't understand what was happening to me.

Matthieu and I celebrated our one-year anniversary while in Kenya. He told me to bring an overnight bag with me to church as we wouldn't be staying at Beatrice and Aggrey's that night. As soon as the service was over, he led me a short distance on foot to the nicest hotel in the city. It was located in a park and had a heated swimming pool and spa. I had been feeling so tired, I asked if he would mind if I took a nap first, even though I was reluctant to miss any part of our overnight stay. He was happy to let me rest and told me the day was mine to do as I pleased; he sat down and opened his book.

When I woke up, I was refreshed. It was too late to take advantage of the spa, so we dressed up for dinner and went to eat in the outdoor terrace. For one night, we forgot we were far from home. We ate a four-course meal next to the exotic plants by the outdoor swimming pool between the torches that lit the terrace. The next day we went for a swim and spent time in the Jacuzzi and spa, returning to our house refreshed that night. It was a really rich and full first year of marriage.

With the shopping, the nice house we were staying in, the safaris, and those idle days at the YMCA during our months in Kenya, I felt like we were doing so little good. I was concerned to see myself grow lazy and selfish and felt guilty that we weren't doing what we came to do, which was serve the poor. On the spur of the moment, I offered up a hasty prayer as I was looking through the racks of clothes at an outdoor market. *God, please help me to be a better servant.*

That night, we came out of the midweek service and walked towards Mary and Eli's car, a couple who offered to take us home. Matthieu went around the front of the car in the dark, and suddenly his voice shot out in pain. When I ran to where he was, I saw him clutching his leg and rocking back and forth, breathing in short gasps. I didn't know what had happened. All I could do was watch him in anguish, knowing he was in pain but that there was nothing I could do.

When he was finally able to speak, he said, "I think I broke my foot. I didn't see the ditch there in the dark."

"Can you walk?" Eli asked. Matthieu shook his head adamantly. So we drove to the hospital where we paid a total of sixteen dollars for the visit, X-ray, painkillers, and crutches. He had indeed broken his foot.

That night, after hovering around Matthieu and fetching various things he might need, I lay down in bed. I heard the guard settling down outside our window for the night. Just when I had gotten completely comfortable and opened my book, Matthieu said, "Oh, sorry. I forgot to get my book over there before getting in bed. Can you get it for me?"

In a burst of impatience, I stood up and walked across the room, giving a huge sigh. I was thinking, "I'm going to be waiting on him, hand and foot, for a long time..."—when, reaching for the book, I turned around suddenly, arrested with that thought.

"Honey," I said. "I didn't tell you this, but I prayed to be a better servant today. And now look. I have to wait on you, hand and foot."

"Ouch," he answered ruefully. "Could you try to be more careful in what you pray for from now on?"

But he laughed with me as I protested, "This was not at *all* what I had in mind."

Although our stay in Nairobi was more of a reprieve than anything else, we did participate in a small number of humanitarian projects. We visited one of the orphanages—our visit too short to do much more than play a few games with the children. They received their meal in obedient lines and ate on lath boards forming a pathway over muddy sewage water. There were big bundles of ragged clothing hanging over the metal walls. The scene reminded me of something I would see in a Dickens novel, and I noticed that even the Hargeisa orphanage was clean by comparison.

The orphans reduced to living on the street—the homeless boys who sniffed glue to get high—were in an even more deplorable state. Many of these children had lost their entire family to AIDS, and what was first a method to forget their troubles, soon became a highly addictive habit that killed their brain cells at a rapid and dangerous pace. There was not a large window for helping these children get out of their situation before help was too late, and there were few structures in place to achieve this. We had no resources to help and found ourselves avoiding them because we couldn't know which of them were dangerous. This made me sad; they were too young to have such empty eyes.

We participated in World AIDS Day, a large rally to educate people about AIDS, and were given a preemptive lesson by a specialist. We learned that AIDS spread throughout the country, in part because African people are more susceptible to certain strains of AIDS, and in part because of the lack of education and superstition in certain areas. After explaining to a group of people, living in a small village, what a condom was and demonstrating how to use it by putting it on a broomstick, the volunteers found that these same people were still contracting AIDS. The error lay in the fact that, while these men did use the condoms, they were putting them on the broomstick and leaning it in the corner of their room while going about their business.

One of the educators struck a nerve when she said to our group, "You are mourning the loss of three thousand people in the attack on the twin towers. But more than that die in Kenya each *week* from AIDS." In the Women's Day at our church, a woman with AIDS spoke bravely and frankly to the large group of mainly Kenyans about this disease—a disease which still carried a stigma and death sentence.

"One out of five people end up dying from AIDS," she said, enunciating each word powerfully. "Look at the two people to your right and the two people to your left. One of them has AIDS...or it's you," she finished, piercing the hearts of her audience. Indeed, in the large local church we attended, deaths were announced every week.

Life in Kenya was raw, in a way. Even if we could enjoy some of the luxuries, it was impossible to escape the desperation. I didn't often go to the Nairobi business district, but one time I was heading back towards the bus station after meeting someone. It was about noon. Suddenly, I felt fingers wrapping around my neck, and I instinctively whirled around, blocking the arm and sending the man cowering away. He had been going after my fake gold necklace, and I could tell he was high on drugs. Later that evening, Matthieu listened to my story, his forehead wrinkling with concern, but he couldn't help but laugh when I demonstrated the Kung fu move I had used.

However, there was nothing amusing about the attack on Malinda. She was descended upon by a gang of men who put a plank under her neck and lifted her off her feet to choke her while they stripped her of everything of value she had. Her neck was still bruised when I saw her a few days later. Ironically, in spite of this terrifying experience, she was the one out of all of us who still said she was, "living her dream." She is working in Africa to this day, married to an Ethiopian man.

There were riots. We listened to a preacher in our church, who ministered in one of the slums, talk about his experience getting his family out of their house. He was part of the minority tribe that was butchered during those riots. When the family was forced out because people were setting fire to it, he was the last one of his family to walk out the door.

In the instant that he turned back to reach his arm in the doorway and grab his bag of papers and valuables, the crowd separated him from his wife and children just ahead. One of the men blocked his way and put a knife to his throat, but the preacher simply looked at him and said, "My brother" in the other man's tribal language. The man let him go, and he was able to rejoin his family. The next day, they crossed many bodies that were mutilated and decapitated.

When sitting at the YMCA one day, I met a woman named Hannah, and we found a table together so we could talk. "I used to be in the ministry in Addis," she said. "But then things got too difficult for me, and I had to come back. I just had no more strength."

"What happened?" I asked her, curious that the ministry could drain her to the point of needing to return.

"Well, I was leading with my friend Dan. We weren't romantically involved, but he was a good friend. Anyway, one day the riots broke out on the streets. A group of us were sitting in my apartment when we got a call that one of the sisters in the church needed to go to the hospital. We decided to help her, in spite of the riots."

"When we got to where the sister lived," she continued, "we found out that she had already gotten help and was on her way to the hospital, so we turned back to go home. There was another brother that had come along with Dan and me. All of a sudden, we heard the sounds of the riot coming down our street. So we escaped down one of the side streets. I was running as fast as I could because I could hear the people getting closer, but Dan and the other brother were still ahead of me."

"Dan slowed down and turned back to help me, reaching his hand out to grab mine and pull me along with him. Just at the moment he turned back, someone shot him in the chest," she said numbly, the misery visible on her face. "He fell to the ground, and there was blood gushing from his chest."

"I'm usually so squeamish," she continued. "Even a small cut on the finger will make me feel sick, but I kneeled next to him, with both hands on his chest, trying to contain the blood that kept gushing out."

"I kept calling out, begging for people to help me, but everyone rushed by and ignored me. He died next to me." I listened silently, waiting for her to continue.

"The strange thing is—Dan had prayed, about a week before he died, that he would live every day as if it were his last. And he really did. Everyone saw the difference in him. He was so close to God that week, and his ministry was on fire."

"Ever since then," she went on, "I can't help but think that there was a spiritual lesson for me there too. When I called out to those people who were running by and completely ignoring me, I keep thinking that this is how other people feel without showing it. You know, I see the faces on the train, and their eyes look so dead, and it feels like they're calling for help just like I was, except without words. It made me want to live differently."

"Anyway," she concluded, "I came back to Nairobi after that." I had no words with which to comfort her when her story was finished; my throat ached, and my eyes were filled with tears. My own life had always been so removed from such danger.

We had been in Nairobi for four months. Mike and Petrina returned to their lives in New York to start a family, and Christian also went back to New York to get married. That left Matthieu and me, Malinda and Kara, and Chris and Henry from South Africa. Most of the other NGOs had returned to Hargeisa and set up base again, so our headquarters decided to send us back.

I was excited to return to where I felt we were really making a difference. But practically speaking, I was nervous about that four-hour flight in an eight-seater aircraft with no toilet. We said goodbye to Beatrice and Aggrey and packed all our bags once again. We headed to the airport where we climbed into the aircraft and buckled ourselves in. It was just Chris, Henry, Matthieu and I. Malinda and Kara planned to come a few days later.

We buckled ourselves into our seats, and the plane bounced off lightly into the air, ascending rapidly and circling over the savannah before heading northeast. As we approached the cruising altitude of fifteen thousand feet, I felt my ears go *pop*, accompanied by a strange sensation. It wasn't the normal *pop* that occurred after yawning in high altitudes.

I glanced ahead at the two pilots and saw there was a red light blinking on the dashboard. I looked over at Matthieu with wide eyes and discovered he was already looking at me. "Something's wrong," he mouthed. I grew cold with dread.

The pilots were communicating soundlessly with each other through their headsets, and they kept looking back at us as they started a fast descent. We immediately flew back to the runway. When we got off the plane, we learned that the air pressure valve had broken. We would have been in danger of losing oxygen if we hadn't descended to a lower altitude quickly enough.

The mechanics at the airport promised they would be able to fix it, so we meekly stayed put while they worked on the plane. We weren't entirely convinced of its safety but didn't have the courage or problem-solving skills to find another way back to Hargeisa.

Three hours later, they declared the plane to be fixed, so we resumed our places in the aircraft, only to have the air pressure valve break again at fifteen thousand feet. We touched down a second time, convinced it wasn't our day to return to Hargeisa. We stayed in Nairobi for the night with a different couple as we couldn't bear to inconvenience Beatrice and Aggrey, who had already served us more than enough. The next day, we returned to the airport where we got on a different plane and made the flight without a hitch.

We landed on the sandy strip at the airport in Hargeisa, our little plane chasing the goats off the runway as we touched down. We breathed in the dry air as we stepped off the plane and soaked in the friendly and familiar sights. As we turned towards the concrete building that served as an airport, we saw our friends waiting for us, crowding around Abdi Hakim.

He grabbed our bags with his big white smile, showing surprise at Matthieu's crutches, and led the way back to the car. There were only three months left to our stay in Africa, and I couldn't help but feel we were exactly where we were meant to be.

On that day they will say to Jerusalem, "Do not fear, O Zion; do not let your hands hang limp. The Lord your God is with you, he is mighty to save. He will take great delight in you, he will quiet you with his love, he will rejoice over you with singing." Zephaniah 3

17

THE FISH AND THE LOAVES

The essence of our entire year's work in Africa was summed up in that final period in Somaliland. We could have skipped everything else, apart from those short three months, and achieved the same end-result. Everything significant happened at the end.

We made an unpleasant, but necessary, trip to Djibouti to close operations as funding had dramatically decreased, and the organization could no longer support the two countries. The four days we spent in Djibouti were awkward. Here, we had rented this big house and asked to have air conditioning in all the rooms as a special favor. Our Djiboutian landlord knew it would be difficult to replace us and was not keen on letting us go easily. As the niece of a government minister, she added the weight of his position to her own pressure and had us meet at his office. We sat in the anteroom for nearly an hour, which was meant to further intimidate us. It worked, but the facts remained; we simply could not afford to pay the expensive rent any longer.

We also had to let go of our consultant, Ahmed, forcing him to return to his small livelihood. He fought with every argument he could think of, reminding us how disappointed the orphanage and university would be to find out we were leaving without doing anything we had promised, and how we would be losing face with the government after fighting so hard to be established. On the whole, it was a lesson in humility.

We got off the plane in Hargeisa, carrying the remainder of our belongings from Djibouti, and breathed a huge sigh of relief to be back. Since Mike and Petrina had gone home, we took over their larger bedroom, and started putting our things away. As I stacked our shirts in the wardrobe, I felt something hard towards the back of the shelf, and I pulled it into plain view. It was a small stash of toys that had never been put to use.

It wasn't much—some small balls and a jump rope, markers, and a doll. With three hundred and fifty orphans, these toys wouldn't go very far. But I reasoned that the kids had nothing to play with, except bits of glass and the small stones they found in the dirt. Some of them had never seen a toy, much less played with one, and something was better than nothing.

I thought, *why not try to create a playroom in one of the spare rooms, even if it's just with these few toys?* So I asked someone at the orphanage to paint one of the cement rooms in a cheerful color and put mats on the floor, promising we would pay the expenses. They painted the room bright yellow and added blue shelves, and as we watched their progress, our team decided to add another playroom just outside the orphanage that the village children could use. I was eager for the day we could put them to use.

A couple days later, when we were visiting Edna at the hospital, she told us about a charity that had five thousand shoeboxes of toys they wanted to deliver to the children in Somaliland. She was going to oversee the distribution throughout the country, but she wanted us to help distribute the boxes for the orphanage. She brought us with her on her trip to visit the pharmacies near the coast, and there we saw the massive cargo ship with the promised shoeboxes docked at the port.

The boxes were brought to a locked room outside the orphanage, and every couple of days, we brought a truckload to our house to organize. Our job was to sort through all the shoeboxes and remove any religious material (anything denoting Christianity was illegal in the country), remove any expired candy or food, and sort the boxes so they would be given to the appropriately aged children. We also equalized the goodies in the boxes, as some were packed with treats, while others were rather sparse.

The amount of boxes we received far exceeded the three hundred and fifty we would need for the orphans. As we started sorting through the boxes, the pile of toys that would not work for an individual box, but that would be perfect for a playroom, began to grow. In addition, we simply had too many boxes to hand out and began to add the contents of the excess boxes to our pile destined for the playrooms. We had more than enough for both playrooms and then some to stockpile as insurance against the inevitable theft that would occur.

When the day came to distribute the shoeboxes at the orphanage, we sat all of the children down on the ground in groups, according to age. They knew something big was afoot, but I don't think they understood the extent of what was happening. We started pulling the boxes out, one by one, and had the children form lines to come and receive theirs. Some chattered away excitedly, some complained about how the contents of their box were not as good as their neighbor's, and still others just sat there in stunned silence without even removing anything from their box. They had never held a toy before, and here was an entire box of toys, socks, pencils, candy, stickers, toothbrushes…entirely for them.

As I watched them pulling items out and exclaiming over them, or just staring at their boxes in mute amazement, tears fell from my eyes. My husband was also overcome, and it did not take him long to see the spiritual connection between what happened at the orphanage and what had occurred with Jesus' disciples and the baskets of fish and bread.

The disciples wondered how in the world they would ever be able to feed five thousand people. Jesus asked them to focus on what they already had—two loaves of bread and a few fish. What did I have? Just a few small toys that were supposed to meet the needs of an entire orphanage. What did God do? He provided an individual box of treasures to satisfy the needs of each child, with baskets and baskets of supplies left over to fill two playrooms.

We were starting to see positive changes at the orphanage as a result of our work. As a nurse, Malinda collected research to show that the majority of the illnesses and deaths in the orphanage were due to poor sanitation. With her documented cases, a larger NGO was able to acquire funds to install running water, piped in from the desert, so the children could drink clean water and wash their hands after they used the toilets. This was especially crucial considering they only ate with their hands.

I was still active in the nursery at the orphanage. I was shocked to learn that Khadra, the baby I cared for in those first two months in Hargeisa, had died while we were in Kenya. She had started to put on the necessary weight when we fed her with a medicine dropper, and I couldn't comprehend how her death could have happened so soon afterwards. With the language barrier, I never did find out.

But now there was a little baby who was so skinny and small he looked more like a newborn than a nine-month-old baby. He had been left on the doorstep of the orphanage, and no one knew his name or clan. So he was given the name Moguay, which means, "doesn't know his father." He had dysentery and was weak, and I often went over to the orphanage to feed him with the dropper—there was something about him that wrung my heart. I caressed his cheeks and touched his limbs whenever I could, knowing how healing touch can be. I was determined that he would not suffer the same fate as Khadra.

Chris, Henry, and Matthieu decided to have a playground built inside the orphanage grounds, and they drew up the plans and set up the equipment. We also went on an immunization drive, speaking with people living in tents on the outskirts of town and giving them vitamins. We helped the small college set up their website and participated in the international conference on Female Genital Mutilation.

There was no time to teach the nursing students at the hospital anymore. The date for the grand opening was fast approaching, and everyone was working hard to get it ready. I spent a lot of time in a small supply closet, sorting through the hospital materials that had been donated. I threw away the medicine that was long expired but kept certain others that were only recently expired and could still be used. I counted the number of IV bags, sorted the boxes of latex gloves by size, organized the various tubing and needles according to size and purpose, and stockpiled the saline solution. There was an immense amount of donated supplies, but the hospital was not officially opened yet, and we knew the supplies would dwindle all too quickly once it was.

I could see that Edna was working tirelessly to get the medical components of the hospital set up. But we were just under two weeks away from the opening ceremony, and when I walked through the hospital rooms, I saw how far we were from being ready. In the first room I visited, neither the electricity nor plumbing was working. In the next room, the hospital bed was still in pieces and needed to be set up. The room following that hadn't even been painted, and there were buckets of plaster and tools lying about. The rest of my informal survey revealed similar deficiencies in each room. Although the operating theatres were in fairly good shape, there were even some electrical issues there, which could have a big impact if left unresolved.

I looked around and thought, *we have just ten days left, and there are so many things that need to be done. At this rate, it won't be done in time.* I knew how important the grand opening was for Edna and the hospital. All the leading officials had been invited to the opening ceremony and would be given a tour. I went through the hospital, clipboard in hand, and wrote down everything that needed to be done. I estimated roughly how long it would take to do each task and divided the tasks by the number of days. I then presented the foreman with the list and told him I would be by every morning to see what had been accomplished.

It was a pretty cheeky move for someone who had absolutely no authority or construction experience, but it worked. He and his men called me "The General" and met with me every morning as they stuck to the schedule I had created. Pretty soon the sinks in each room had running water, the beds were set up with fresh sheets, and all the debris had been cleaned. By the time the officials were there for the tour, there was no disorder to be ashamed of; everything was perfect.

The hospital was in full swing immediately. The nurses worked long shifts, throwing themselves fully into their jobs and learning much more there than they did in the classroom. Soon women were coming in from the surrounding areas to deliver their babies, and the overall mortality rate in the area declined significantly.

But there was still loss. One day we drove up to the hospital to the sight of an older woman wailing at the gate. Abdi Hakim leapt out of the car and ran over to her, conferring with her through her sobs. We learned that it was his aunt, and his cousin had just died of eclampsia. She hadn't been taking her medicine correctly and had gone into a coma before passing away. We gave him the car, and the weekend off, and found a ride home with another driver.

The hospital had their first overseas doctors who came from the UK to donate their time for a few weeks, training the staff and giving medical care to the local people. They had been there just a day or two when one of the orphanage workers hurried over to our compound early in the morning.

"Moguay is very sick," she said, out of breath. "You need to take him to the hospital."

I took one look at her face and said, "We'll go right away."

Abdi Hakim had just arrived, and I let him know what was happening as I ran to get my bag. We rushed over to the orphanage where I grabbed Moguay and held him close to me in my arms, talking to him as we drove to the hospital. "Darling you're going to grow up to be big and strong—you're going to be okay. You're going to make it." His eyes were clear, and his gaze didn't leave my face. I could almost imagine he wasn't sick, if it weren't for his breath coming in short gasps.

As soon as we got there, I rushed inside and was taken straight to the British doctors. One of them examined him quickly. She consulted a book, alternately studying remedies for dehydration and dysentery and giving orders to the hospital aides. "Prepare boiled water and cool it off, put X amount of sugar and salt in it."

Then she turned to me, and said, "His veins are too weak for an IV. We need to get him hydrated right away. Once we get the mixture, you need to give it to him a little at a time."

However, the hospital aide had trouble understanding her English and prepared the mixture wrong. The doctor was overwhelmed by the conditions, I think, and tried to rein in her frustration as she asked the aide do it again properly. Never was time more of the essence than for little Moguay. The aide went back and finally got the mixture right.

I fed him a tiny bit at a time with a medicine dropper, but he kept flooding his diapers with diarrhea and coughing from pneumonia. The doctor watched over my shoulder as I changed him and continued to feed him. "I have to tell you, it doesn't look good," she said.

But I believed. I had been keeping a special eye out for him since we arrived back in Hargeisa, so he *had* to make it. I prayed. What else was I there for, if not that? I kept feeding him the mixture, holding him, kissing his forehead and talking to him, "You're going to make it. You're going to stay alive. You're going to grow up." He continued to fix his eyes on me as if he were absorbing my every expression, my lips, my smiles.

It seemed like no time at all had passed before Abdi Hakim came into the room to tell me it was time to go back for lunch. My mind was busy. I was thinking about how I could set up a place in my room so I could take care of Moguay for a few days until he got strong enough. There was no question of his sleeping at the orphanage while he was this weak. I regretted that it was not permitted to adopt the orphans if one wasn't both Somali and Muslim. Regretfully, I handed Moguay over to the nurse so I could figure out what needed to be done.

The instant he left my arms and was taken by the nurse, his tiny body went into convulsions. Rooda, the head nurse, who had become a good friend, quickly took him from the nursing student and brought him over to the table where she administered mouth-to-mouth and CPR to his tiny ribcage. I stood there in shock. *This can't be happening*, I thought. From the depth of my own ribcage came a silent wail. *Nooooooooo!*

This went on for maybe a minute, maybe two. Then she shook her head, turned to me and said, "I'm sorry Jennie," as she laid her hand on my arm.

Tears were streaming down my face as she washed his body and wrapped it in a clean white cloth to be buried—the nicest clothing he had ever worn. Then she handed him to me, and I went numbly down the stairs and walked over to take my place in the back seat of the truck. I barely looked at the small bundle I held loosely in my arms, heavier in death than he had been in life. Abdi Hakim stole glances at my face in the rearview mirror as he drove.

When we arrived at the orphanage, one of the other workers took him from my arms as she kept up a cheerful exchange with Abdi Hakim. Then she walked away with the body to bring him out back to be buried. As we were still sitting there, Dowood came up to me and started pestering me about getting computers for the orphanage again.

"Not now, Dowood," I said.

He looked at me in surprise. "Jennie…do you cry?"

A fresh wave of grief swept over me, and I nodded my head mutely in quiet sobs.

"But why?" he asked.

"Because Moguay's dead," I finished with a wail.

"Teacher," he said. "Don't cry. It's only an orphan."

When I got home, Matthieu held me in his arms, speaking tender words as I cried quietly. "Moguay will remember you as the person who was always smiling down at him. Somebody loved him on this earth," he emphasized. "At least he had someone who loved him."

That afternoon, Dowood came to our compound and told our teammate Kara, "Other NGOs give us food and supplies, but now I know that you love us because Jennie cried when Moguay died."

My heart was turned over and ploughed through with grief for a long time after I lost baby Moguay—for I did feel as if it were *I* that lost him. But as I tried to process everything, I came to believe that God arranged for Dowood to be there at that moment to see me cry, so he could see that the loss of an orphan was something worth crying over —and through it, he too might feel loved.

As our sabbatical drew to an end, we finally witnessed rain on desert soil. At first just a few drops started to fall, which brought us eagerly to the porch. Then the rain came more steadily until it was thundering down. Chris quickly went inside to heat up the chai tea and then brought a mug out to each of us. We sat on the open porch with hot, spicy tea in our hands, smelling the damp earth and listening to the rain fall. Soon the earth was no longer thirsty, and the sky grew quiet.

I asked Abdi Hakim to accompany me to the market in town so I could buy the nicest, most expensive Muslim cap to give to a friend of mine. I asked him to choose the most beautiful *koofiyad* he could find, stressing that this friend of mine really deserved the best. He obliged, choosing an expensive white one that was laced with silver embroidery.

On our last day in Somaliland, we climbed out of the truck filled with luggage representing our one-year stay in Africa—suitcases and bags stuffed to the brim with incense, goat stools, etched wooden bowls, and dyed cloths. We had already said goodbye to our friends at the orphanage and hospital. Now we stood facing Abdi Hakim. He had been our protector and friend.

He shook my hand, though I was a woman and a foreigner, and I handed him a parcel carefully wrapped in white tissue paper. The *koofiyad*. I watched as he took it, not daring to open it but surely knowing what it was. He nodded his head fiercely and yelled at some boys in beautiful, guttural Somali to come and take our bags, hiding his emotions behind his gruff voice.

We stepped into the aircraft that would take us to Addis Ababa and then on to our final destination. The brown sands stretching over this country we had come to know, the small brown mountain peppered with green shrubs, the concrete buildings and houses, not one untouched by the bombing and shelling of civil war—all these things became smaller and smaller until they were no more.

We are hard pressed on every side, but not crushed; perplexed, but not in despair; persecuted but not abandoned; struck down but not destroyed. Second Corinthians 4

18

THE YEAR OF WEEPING

I didn't know it, but the year following Africa would become "the year of weeping." What should have been a sweet reunion with our friends and church quickly turned to heartache. Almost nothing went the way we would have it.

Matthieu wasn't able to fly back with me to New York because of his green card application process. We flew to Ethiopia together where he bought a plane ticket to France on standby and prepared to wait for the next available flight. He told me to wait for him at the airport hotel, and if he wasn't able to get on the plane that night he would meet me there. It was fortunate for him that he got on the first plane going to France that same night, but it didn't feel fortunate to me. It was a wretchedly lonely feeling, after everything we had been through, to wait alone in a foreign hotel room for a husband who would not come back.

Betsy's husband, Nerses, picked me up at JFK airport when I arrived early in the morning. He then went off to work, leaving me to shower and sleep in their Murray Hill apartment. The shower had a steady, hot jet stream of water, and the soaps and shampoos were wonderfully scented. It was my first shower like it in a year, and I trembled as I dried myself off with the thick, white towel. I quickly fell asleep on the couch and didn't hear the phone ringing at all, only waking up to the door buzzer as my friend Pamela came to visit and officially welcome me back.

New York had changed. It was hard to believe that the psyche of an entire city could change overnight, especially that of a tough, old broad like New York; but it did after September 11th. My old roommate, Sue, told me in her soft voice, "You have no idea what it was like here after 9/11. You could smell smoke for weeks all over Manhattan."

The people had changed; they no longer possessed the cocky air of one who was going places and knew it. When I escaped by mere minutes from being trapped in a Midtown elevator for twelve hours during the blackout of 2003, the entire city was in an uproar. The traffic had come to a complete standstill and the trains weren't running. As I joined the mass exodus of people walking fifty blocks downtown, I saw a young woman standing in the middle of the street, weeping into her cell phone. "It's another terrorist attack. I don't know what to do." Proud New York had become like a skittish colt, looking askance, and trusting no one. Nobody was sure of anything anymore.

While Matthieu was still in France trying to get home, I started setting up the apartment that his old roommate had been subletting while we were gone. The next week, I went to my first and only interview. All the business clothes I had pulled out of storage were now too small, so I had to go out and buy an interview suit. I found a copy of my most recent résumé, which was up to date, except for the year I had spent in Africa. I hoped that it would be overlooked since I knew the person hiring.

My old boss—the executive at the bank, whose assistant position I only took because God answered every reluctant prayer I flung up to Him—had since changed jobs to head a local branch of an Indian company. He held off from hiring anyone for the Executive Assistant role until I had returned from Africa, so he could give the position to me. I didn't realize this at the time, but the City was in a major recession, and I would need this job more than I could have predicted.

Being an Eastern European man and not one for subtlety, he made a joking comment about my weight gain, which I chose to let slide because we were friends, and I knew what to expect from him. But I was still deeply embarrassed. I had almost hoped that the extra twenty-five pounds didn't show all that much but had been foolish to think it. I was determined to get back to my old weight and familiar clothes as quickly as possible. I would have been destroyed to learn that instead of getting better over the years, it would only get worse.

I liked the new place where I worked. We were on Park Avenue and Fortieth Street, two blocks from Grand Central Station. My desk was on the far wall with a view on the rest of the brightly lit office, and the windows to the side overlooked Park Avenue. I quickly adjusted to my new schedule.

Matthieu's green card paperwork came through after one month in France, and he came home. As soon as I saw him, I threw myself into his arms, and we held each other tightly. It seemed almost miraculous that I had him back again. Like skittish New York, I wasn't sure of anything either.

Once Matthieu was home, we were asked to visit some of the ministries in our church to share our experiences in Africa. We went to Harlem, Staten Island, and our own ministry in Manhattan. As soon as I stepped up to the microphone to speak, I began to cry before I could even utter one word. The collective horrors of what I had seen, felt dimly through a protective shield of denial, combined with the suffering of my bewildered New York friends had brought an onslaught of sorrow.

I noticed our church had started to change. I had heard whispers of discontent from the e-mails I received overseas, but I was protected from the brunt of it by being physically removed. Almost as soon as we returned from Africa, one of the ministers serving in a church overseas wrote a letter that was meant for the other ministry staff. Instead someone distributed it on the worldwide web, and every member of the assembly devoured it.

As harsh as the letter was, it showed a clear need for repentance, using Jesus' words to call the leadership "whitewashed tombs—clean and sparkly on the outside, but on the inside full of death." Actually what he said was that they were *worse* since they didn't even try to hide their sins. Instead, they wore their pride and self-importance openly for everyone to see. Although it was unfair as a blanket assessment, it revealed the need to address the way the church was run.

The backlash was appalling. Young couples who had been trusted members of the ministry for years were suddenly quitting and moving away, making those members who wanted to work through the problems feel strangely insecure. Members of the congregation held meetings to discuss all the wrongs they had suffered under an arrogant leadership. Some of the ministers apologized again and again, but the meetings came close to turning into lynch mobs. Those who were earnest in their desire to listen, change, and repent became exhausted by the incessant criticism. One of the full-time staff suffered a heart attack from stress, and his family moved to the sister church in Florida.

Some people were so relieved they didn't need to submit to the oppression of the church anymore, they rushed off and got divorced, got involved in their old lifestyles, started using substances again, and often behaved worse than they did before. Others simply found that the church didn't work for them, and they left to pursue their faith elsewhere. Although many of the friendships forged in the church were able to withstand the differing opinions and opposing choices, there were some who cut off all ties with anyone who stayed in the church, no matter how close the relationship had been. About a tenth of us stayed in place to work things out and help in whatever way we could. Where else were we going to go? This was our family.

One of the main accusations was the high salaries that some of the ministers earned—salaries set by an independent accounting firm with full access to the church finances, and who based the figures on other churches of comparable size. In retrospect, I don't think the figures were that shocking. But when you thought about the single mom striving to put food on the table while tithing to please God, the salary disproportion between the leaders and some of the flock seemed wrong.

People also wanted to change the practice of discipling—the fact that everyone in the church was assigned a "discipling partner" to meet with once a week to help them grow in their faith. In principal, it was a great idea, and also a Biblical one. Personally, I learned so much from being discipled and from discipling others, even if it was nothing more than how to grow in humility and allow myself to be taught by someone I didn't always initially respect. But problems occurred when there was someone like me, who was given this responsibility before I had the maturity in my faith to handle it. In doing so, I bruised people's hearts and faith by discipling them too harshly.

I think what saved our church in Manhattan from completely dissolving was the humility and openness of one couple in particular —a couple with whom I'm still close. The husband had already apologized for all the ways he was insensitive and had sinned against people, and it was evident his apology was sincere.

He told us what he was earning from the church and said, "I can continue to work in the full-time ministry, but if we need to lower the salary, I can only do it on a part-time basis because I need to support my family. I can also leave the ministry and get a different job. Either way, I'm not leaving you guys."

This speech was healing, and our ministry grew close and protective as a result. Pretty soon we became the remnant, and others arrived from the various fallen ministries in Manhattan. Together we formed something akin to a raw band of survivors. In the end, this couple did serve in the full-time ministry for several years before finally stepping down. He ended up with a terrific job in his chosen field pre-ministry, and they are still in New York serving the church.

What happened to my church was a shock. I mean—a shock. I was blind and only saw the good in the way the church was run. After all, it had done so much good for me, personally. I couldn't understand why people were so unforgiving. My devotion to the church stemmed from having been able to change my life with its help. I also came to know and understand the Bible on my own, without needing a pastor to explain it to me. And we were family. This was not a place where you showed up on Sundays then went off in obscurity for the rest of the week. All of these seemed to be the fundamental elements of a church.

When I saw people who were family to me walk away and completely cut ties with everyone, including me, I didn't even recognize them anymore. It was like having a husband who changed overnight, leaving you bewildered, abandoned, and betrayed to the core. It felt like divorce.

Between the church collapse and my inability to lose the extra weight, I was struggling with a great deal of anxiety. The feelings of worthlessness I'd had since childhood became pronounced, and I started to envision hurting myself. I didn't actually want to carry it out, but whenever the anxiety built up to a pressure point, I would imagine being shot in the head, or stabbing myself in the chest, and somehow these images lessened the anxiety. I decided that I needed to see a therapist because I didn't know how to untangle the threads of depression and disappointment that had become so knotted.

I had gone through therapy before—the counselor in Taiwan, the Christian counselor in Paris, and again while I was in Chemical Recovery. But I didn't like therapy. I grew bored talking about myself each week.

I also didn't like to sit in uncomfortable emotions, and I rarely let myself fully grieve. Any time I talked about painful events, it was accompanied by silent tears, which rolled down my cheeks as I tried to control my breaking voice. Matthieu called it "oozing." The pain overflowed to the point where it oozed out of my eyes, the only outward sign of a turbulent heart. I oozed a lot when I came back from Africa, especially when I talked about Moguay.

But after the church breakup, I truly wept out loud for the first time in my adult life. Pamela, the one who had welcomed me when I returned from Africa, cut off contact with me when the church split apart—she, who had recently become a significant part of my life. She had spent a year being angry at the injustices in the church, but I had been so separated from it, I couldn't match her feelings when I returned. When she expressed her anger venomously, I viewed the minister in question as the victim and told her the problems stemmed from her own anger. Not surprisingly, our friendship ended shortly afterwards.

That was when Matthieu saw me really cry for the first time—when he saw me fully let go, holding me as I convulsed in loud guttural sobs. I think these tears were the culmination of everything: the pain of 9/11, of Africa, of the church, even my own disappointment with my life. I didn't expect that I would have the wedding of a princess, only to immediately gain a lot of weight—to go from a life of adventure, only to be stuck in a mundane job, and then be part of a ministry that was falling apart. I was supposed to be covered in the glory of God. Where had He gone, and on whom was He now shining His face? It wasn't me.

"I'm just a fat, middle-aged secretary," I wailed one day while standing near the apartment door. Someone in the hallway cleared his throat as he waited for the elevator. I sunk my face in my hands, deeply embarrassed—he must have heard what I said.

There was other tension in our lives that ensured I would remain in therapy for a year. The work environment in my new job started to become stressful. I liked what I was doing, but was pulled in too many directions. For one thing, I was no longer the sole assistant to my boss; I was also working for the chairman and CEO whenever they were in the country.

And even though my official title was Executive Assistant, I became responsible for work orders that came in. Then Human Resources handed me some of the payroll because I already knew how to do it, and there were many different types of visas for each expat category—too much for their department alone. In addition, I had to start setting up work permits for the company in each individual state so the foreign employees could conduct business in those states as well. My to-do list was pages long, and I had two racks of files on my desk that needed attention.

Everybody was so desperate to get their work done they leaned on me for help. At first, I sympathized with their predicament, but I soon started snapping at people on the phone when they asked for things. I became that bureaucratic person who simply doesn't care. "Look. You'll get the work order when you get it. My first priority is the CEO, not your work order."

I had no compassion and no scruples about saying no, or, if truth were told, about saying "screw you," even if it was only in my head. My boss, who had known me in my idyllic world before Africa and the church breakup, looked at me with something of a sneer as he shook his head. "You've changed, Jennie. You're a different person. I'm not even sure you're still a Christian."

All I could think was that I wanted to quit, to run away, to find some way of relieving the pressure. But I couldn't quit because Matthieu, who had taken up his old job at Hewlett Packard, was laid off a mere month after his return. It happened during the massive layoffs at the company under new direction. Although he suspected it might happen because he saw the trend, nothing quite prepared him for how hard it would be.

He confessed that his first thought was, "I'll show them. I'll take my severance package and put it into savings and get a new job in two weeks. Maybe I'll take a little time off first before going somewhere else where they'll really appreciate me."

A year later, he was still unemployed.

All this time, we were, perhaps foolishly, trying to get pregnant because I was thirty-two and he was thirty-four. Each month, the little square on the pink stick came up depressingly empty.

"For I know the plans I have for you," declares the Lord, "plans to prosper and not to harm you, plans to give you a hope and a future." Jeremiah 29

19

THE WALL OF JERICHO

Things got a little worse before they got better. There wasn't a specific event that happened to upset our precarious balance, there was just time chipping away at our courage as we got up each day and faced a reality that showed no promise of changing. Time eroded our patience and magnified the shortcomings we saw in each other and ourselves. The dates from the pull-off calendar floated lazily downward in succession, the little white squares sweeping back and forth, reluctantly obeying gravity.

I had already looked for another job, confident I would find one less stressful and more highly paid, but I had never looked for a job in a recession before. Matthieu's job search was a continuously fruitless endeavor as he received one rejection after another.

Few jobs were available that called for the computer languages in which he was highly skilled. There was one job posting, but it was located in Omaha, Nebraska, and that was absolutely out of the question.

At first, Matthieu went about looking for a new job as if it *were* a job. He got up, got dressed, read the Bible, then hunted for jobs, preparing and sending out cover letters and his CV. But as the months went by and he wasn't seeing any new opportunities, he started to despair. I once arrived home after a stressful day at work to find Matthieu watching *Columbo* reruns, the laundry still undone.

At the lowest point, he was called in for a preliminary interview with a recruitment agency. The agent came bustling in businesslike, sat down, and asked him one technical question. Matthieu answered it. The agent gathered his papers and stood back up.

"Well, I don't think this is going to work out," he said. "But thanks for coming in."

Matthieu was too shocked to say a word even though he was sure he had answered the question correctly. When he got home, he checked the answer he had given, and it had been correct.

I tried to combat my feelings of helplessness by looking for jobs for him in my spare time. Not only were they wide of the mark, but my trying to help gave him a greater sense of despair as if he weren't doing enough. He started to dread my coming home when I would ask him, "But what did you do all day?"

Although we were under pressure, some things occurred during this period that showed us our needs were being taken care of. The first was the fact that I had a job waiting for me when I returned from Africa so we didn't have to undergo both of us being unemployed. The second was our living situation.

A government program had been put in place to encourage people to move back to the lowest part of Manhattan—Battery Park City—which had to be evacuated and gutted for the year following 9/11 because there was so much dust and debris, broken windows, smoke, and asbestos particles filling the air. It was a war zone.

Once the area had been cleaned up, the government wanted to encourage people to return, stimulating the economy and bringing some life back into the tip of Manhattan. Many people were reticent because of the trauma they had experienced while living there. My friend Marie, for example, was alone with her twin babies in their high-rise apartment when she saw the first massive airplane fly right by her window towards the World Trade Center.

I thought the government grant was too good to be true, but one Saturday morning, we took the subway down to South Street Ferry and got out. It was a beautiful summer day with a hot sun and cool breeze, and a bright blue sky filled with fluffy white clouds. It was impossible to imagine that anything bad had ever happened here.

As we walked from the subway, we saw a twisted metal structure that had been put in place—the sphere that once sat in the World Trade Center. Its deformity was the only reminder of what had been destroyed. We headed towards Robert Wagner Park, which I had always thought to be one of the most beautiful places in Manhattan. But I had never explored further up from there into Battery Park City.

That day I discovered that this area was indeed as beautiful as Robert Wagner Park, and perhaps even more so. The buildings were all luxury accommodations, with doormen, and windows overlooking the river. The boardwalk extending along the area led to a marina where the cafés bordered the financial center and the excavation site of the former World Trade Center. In my eight years of living in Manhattan, I had no idea a place like this existed. We stopped in each residential building and got a card from the doorman so we could contact the managers who rented out rooms.

On Monday, I called the first card on the pile, having no idea which building it was, and learned that the government grant was indeed a reality, making the apartments even cheaper than what we were currently paying.

"I'm happy to take down your information," he said. "But there's already a long waiting list. I'll have to add your name to the list."

Without a second thought I asked him, "What would it take for us to skip the waiting list and be first in line to get an apartment?"

"Well," he said thoughtfully, "you could sign for an apartment without having seen it first."

"Okay, we'll do it," I immediately responded. My nonplussed husband went to the rental agent's office the next morning to sign the papers. It was the second building we visited, the one right on the river, which Matthieu had thought would be too luxurious for us to afford.

The day I walked into the apartment for the first time was the day we moved in. Matthieu stayed behind to oversee the movers from our old apartment, and I went ahead on my own. The day was sunny and gorgeous, and when I opened the door to our new apartment, I faced a clean, spacious living room with an open kitchen, white walls, and wooden floors. I walked over to the window and noticed the central air-conditioning, which I switched on. The apartment, the area, the view was all so peaceful and pleasant I just wanted to laugh with joy.

Matthieu was close to his aunt Christine and had spent a few summers visiting her when he was a teen. She lived in Cusco, Peru, devoting her life and income to the poor. She also gave generously to her nephews, and when she found out Matthieu was out of work, she sent us some money. Her gift, combined with the reduced rent, Matthieu's severance package, and some Christmas money from my family spared us from ever having any financial worries that year. In fact, the year Matthieu was out of work, we were living in the nicest part of Manhattan in a luxury rental, and we had more money at our disposal than we'd ever had before.

As the months passed with no change, we finally had no choice but to surrender to our new reality. I began to try harder at my job and appreciate the fact that at least I had one. I continued to go to therapy and work through what I was feeling about the church, and we continued to serve and give our hearts there. Matthieu began to take odd computer jobs, no matter how trivial they were. And I decided to go to the doctor about the fact that I was having trouble getting pregnant.

My new doctor's office was close to my work place. After examining me, he said, "Well, we don't usually start to look for alternative treatments until you've been trying for over a year, but why don't we have both you and your husband checked out to make sure there are no obvious problems. If everything's fine, we'll get you some Clomid. It's a fertility drug." Thankful to have something to do, we started going through the tests to get that part of our lives moving forward.

Matthieu still needed a job. One day he was staring out our bay window, which overlooked Wall Street in the distance, when suddenly he was struck by a thought and prayed, "Come on God—you're *God*. This City is *yours*. You can totally give me a job. You can even give me a job in one of those buildings I can see from here."

That's when he decided to go to war like Joshua did—to walk around Lower Manhattan seven times and pray. That's what God had ordered Joshua to do to bring down the walls of Jericho. Not fight, not take out their swords—walk around the city seven times.

Matthieu put his sneakers on one morning and started walking. Then he did the same thing each day for six more days. On the last time around, his friend Rob came with him. As they came full circle and ended the long march, they stood on the Boardwalk, overlooking the Hudson River and shouted, just like Joshua did.

"AAAAAAAAAAAAAAAAAAAAAHHHHHHHHHHHHHH!"

"Were there people around?" I asked smiling, knowing my quiet soul of a husband, who hated to stand out in a crowd.

"Yup," he grinned.

"What did you do then?" I asked.

He shrugged his shoulders, still grinning. "We went home."

There was no new offer the next day, but his attitude changed. It became more faithful, more along the lines of—okay I don't have a job now, but there is nothing I can do about it other than look for one. The rest is in God's hands.

Over the year, we kept coming back to that job in Omaha, Nebraska and laughing about it. But it got to the point where we stopped laughing and considered it. We even called the ministry there to see what life was like. We finally decided to take the plunge. The day Matthieu submitted his résumé for the job in Nebraska, he got a response saying, "I'm sorry, but we just hired someone today."

Matthieu's colleague had contacted him about job openings in her company a year ago, which he ignored thinking he wasn't a good fit. They were going through another round of hiring, and she sent him a second email. Over the year, he had been studying some of the software applications he wasn't familiar with, and this time he didn't turn her away. He nervously submitted his résumé, including those new proficiencies at the bottom.

When he was called for an interview, he had learned the material so well the interviewer said he was actually more qualified for the senior position at twenty thousand dollars more than he had been making at his previous job, along with a great bonus. He went on three more nerve-racking interviews, and then…

"Matthieu got a job," I yelled out to my entire office when he called with the news. Everyone cheered.

When he went to sign the contract, he looked out the window of his new office across the streets of lower Manhattan. There, in the distance, he saw our little apartment building with our window on the ninth floor, and he smiled to himself. So God did find him a job in one of the buildings that he could see from our window.

A few weeks later, I planned a trip to Los Angeles to visit my old roommate Neyra and my friend Kathy. Before leaving, I took a pregnancy test. As usual, it was negative. But this time I had filled the prescription of Clomid and only needed to wait until I got my period to start taking it. Things were falling into place.

The week in Los Angeles was a healing vacation after a stressful year. While Neyra was at work, I swam laps in her apartment pool on the balcony, feeling my body stretch for the first time in a long time. I lay sleepily in the sun, alone, and felt the warm breeze on my drying skin, my muscles slowly relaxing. At night, we went out to restaurants and visited the beaches and the city. By the time I got back, I was completely relaxed and ready to start work again. Matthieu was thoroughly invigorated to be doing a job he loved. We were back in equilibrium in our marriage, and our smiles came readily.

When I woke up for work on Monday morning, I was impatient to discover I had not yet gotten my period and was therefore unable to start taking Clomid. Then it suddenly dawned on me. Wait—I had already taken a pregnancy test before going to Los Angeles and it was negative, but I was starting to be late. Really late. Maybe I should take another one. Maybe…could I be…?

I quietly grabbed one of the tests from the hallway cupboard and disappeared into the bathroom. As I was about to step into the shower, I saw the faintest pink line appearing in the little square, but I looked away before I could know for sure. This was too great for me to process all at once. I scrubbed shampoo into my hair, soaped, and rinsed off quickly.

But when I stepped out of the shower, the pink line, while still faint, was now clearly visible. After almost a year of trying, we were having a baby. After a year of sorrow and anger and confusion and hardship, there would be new life. This miracle was happening now without Clomid or any other delay.

I walked out of the bathroom where Matthieu, who was about to say, "Your toast is burnt," was stopped short by my expression. He only managed to get one word out of the sentence before he saw the look on my face and the little pink stick in my hand. "Your—"

And I—my gaze fixed on his face, my voice trembling with emotion—finished it for him: "Pregnant."

"Can a mother forget the baby at her breast and have no compassion on the child she has borne? Though she may forget, I will not forget you! See, I have engraved you on the palms of my hands; your walls are ever before me."
Isaiah 49

20

MOTHERHOOD

The beautiful pregnant glow I was waiting for finally showed up in the ninth month, although I was still throwing up even then—every single day, including into the basin beside my labor bed.

My crowning moment of glory was upon our return from a Christmas visit to Paris. We came into our building, having just endured an eight-hour flight and a lurching taxi ride back from Queens, when Matthieu said, "I'm just going to check the mail." Knowing what was coming, I nodded my head with my teeth clenched tight and indicated I was going straight up.

When the elevator doors opened and Matthieu stepped out onto our floor, loaded down with our luggage, his vision was assaulted by the trail of contents from my purse, littering the hallway, and the contents of my stomach all over the rug, wall, and door.

"I couldn't find my keys," I wailed.

By the ninth month, the nausea had lessened, and my aversion to sweets and constant throwing up resulted in a mere twelve-pound weight gain overall. I was able to smile throughout my baby shower, lovingly tie the pink elephant baby bumper around the hand-me-down crib, and wash and fold all the tiny baby clothes in anticipation of the newborn to fill them.

On the morning that marked forty weeks, I woke up with wet underwear and assumed some of my water must have leaked. I called the hospital and was told to come in that evening if my contractions didn't bring me in beforehand. I went to church full of excitement and told all my friends I would be having a baby that day. During the service, my baby seemed calm and didn't move as much as usual during the songs. "She's preparing herself too," I thought.

By early evening, my contractions had started lightly, just enough to make me uncomfortable. We hailed a taxi heading up the West Side Highway, and before long, were stuck in stand-still traffic as minutes turned into an hour. I was trying to contain my panic because I didn't know how quickly the contractions might become urgent, and I had no interest in giving birth in the backseat of a New York taxi. The driver finally made a few ingenious, and possibly illegal, moves and we managed to go up a parallel street with Matthieu glancing over at me anxiously, putting his hand over mine.

At the hospital, I had all the usual exams. When the results came in, the intern looked up from his clipboard and said, "Your water did leak, but only slightly. However we will be keeping you because you have pre-eclampsia. Your blood pressure is high, and we need to get the baby out as soon as possible. We're going to induce your labor and give you medication that will prevent the condition from getting worse."

"Okay, so I won't get sent home?" I asked cautiously. "I'm having my baby now?"

"You won't get sent home," the intern confirmed with a smile.

They brought me to a cheerful room with paintings on the wall and a TV in the corner where I would be laboring and giving birth. I wanted to connect with the contractions before numbing the pain, so I told them to hold off on the epidural. When the contractions came, I bore them silently, unable to talk. When there was a pause in between, I focused on centering my mind and gathering my strength. After a few hours, the contractions became more urgent, which frightened me, and I timidly asked Matthieu to tell the nurse I wanted the epidural. Thirty minutes later, a skinny, drawn woman, who looked more like a heroin addict than an anesthesiologist, finally made her way to my room and spent the next half-hour inserting the needle in my spine. But she got it right, and my mounting panic started to subside as a numbing sensation came over me. I looked at Matthieu and managed a smile. It was nearly three in the morning.

By seven o'clock, the sun was filling the room in warm strips through the half-closed blinds. I was groggy but had been unable to sleep with the fetal monitor, the catheter, the blood pressure cuffs, and all the beeping. The nurse bustled in to check my progress. "You're about eight centimeters, but the baby's heartbeat is a little irregular," she said. "We're still okay for now, but if you don't get further along in the next two hours, we're going to have to do a C-section because we need to get the baby out."

When the intern came back two hours later, she said, "The room for the C-Section won't be ready for another hour. Let's see if you've advanced at all." After giving me a cursory examination, she added, "Why don't I see if I can't help you along," and I felt the corresponding tugs and pressure, and something almost like pain under the blanket of numbness.

In less than an hour, her intervention had worked. "It's time to start pushing," the nurse on my left said. I looked at her with wide eyes, thinking "Push what? I don't feel anything."

The doctor had come in and stood on my right-hand side, "You need to get this baby out pretty quickly if you don't want to have a C-section," she said. "I won't let you push for more than two hours because it will put the baby at risk." I looked at *her* with wide eyes and thought, "Hours? If I don't get this baby out in ten minutes I won't have any strength left to push." The nurse and Matthieu planted themselves on each side of me as the doctor took her place in front.

I knew it was a girl and had desperately wanted one. Matthieu was the oldest in a family of five boys, and three of his brothers had already had sons. I wanted to have the first girl in two generations, and twenty minutes later, I did. My Juliet was born—a delicately featured baby, whose eyes darted around, bright and alert like a bird.

After the nurses got me tidied me up and into a new gown, I felt several warm rushes of blood follow. They changed the sheets, then immediately afterwards, another rush of blood soaked the clean bedding. The doctor kept me in the labor room, finally deciding the loss was not enough to warrant a transfusion, but I needed to stay in emergency care for twenty-four hours following the birth, without eating or drinking anything. Stashed away in a tiny room, I was hooked up to a blood pressure monitor and feet and leg braces, all of which contracted painfully on a regular basis. I couldn't move without a tug from the IV, the catheter or the heart monitors. I barely slept for a second night.

As Matthieu was visiting Juliet in the nursery that evening, he noticed that she suddenly turned blue for a few seconds before returning to her original color. He called for some help and Juliet obligingly turned blue again for the doctor, who immediately placed her under observation in the NICU for thirty-six hours. So Matthieu rushed from one emergency care to the other to keep an eye on his two girls. A nurse kindly took a Polaroid of him holding Juliet and set it on my nightstand, so I could stare at her and believe she was really here.

When I was finally wheeled in to hold my daughter for the first time after twenty-four hours, I wept and wept with her in my arms. I thought, *this is it. There is only one reason I'm alive, and now I know what it is.*

My hospital stay ended a day earlier than Juliet's. I was weepy, weak, and indecisive about whether or not I should stay for that extra night. I felt so guilty leaving her in the hospital without me there, but I didn't feel physically strong enough to sleep on a foldaway bed and do nighttime feedings. So I went home with Matthieu and promised the nurses I'd come early the next morning to feed her.

That night we both collapsed into bed as soon as we got home. Matthieu fell asleep right away, but I wasn't feeling well, and when I went to use the bathroom, I lost a great deal of blood again. It terrified me, and I couldn't understand why my heart was beating so fast. I was in a panic, afraid of having a heart attack.

I wasn't thinking straight; I didn't dare wake Matthieu up and bother him. I was afraid to return to the hospital, afraid to stay home. *God, please don't let me die*, I begged, silently. *What will happen to Juliet and Matthieu? I can't leave them alone. I must stay alive.* Somehow I managed to calm my heart rate and fall asleep.

The next morning at the hospital, I explained what had happened and asked to see a doctor. But I couldn't reenter the maternity ward as I had already been released, and the NICU staff couldn't do anything to help me.

They offered a half-hearted suggestion that I go down to the ER and wait there. Everything was so overwhelming I was unable to make a decision; Matthieu did not know what was wrong with me, so he didn't know whether or not to insist. Finally a nurse came and said that a doctor would alert Labor and Delivery that I was coming back. He would be my referral.

When we went, the L&D nurse looked puzzled and said, "We didn't get a referral about you, and I don't know any doctor by that name." But after checking with someone inside, she came back out and said, "Okay. We'll see you." I wondered if the referring doctor had been an angel.

My blood pressure was high. Usually pre-eclampsia is resolved by giving birth, but it wasn't so in my case. So I was hooked up to machines once more, and instead of being able to feed my baby as planned before taking her home, I was once again separated from her. I was also given two unpleasant internal exams to see if there was a reason I was still losing an excess of blood.

The intern kept asking me, "Are you stressed?" Finally I snapped at her and said, "Yes I'm stressed. No one will tell me why I'm here, and no one will let me see my baby."

I think she really looked at me then for the first time. She sat down beside my examining table and took the time to explain that my blood pressure was dangerously high and that they were trying to lower it with medication. If it worked, I would be able to leave the hospital the same day with my baby.

We did eventually get to leave by the end of the day, although I was weak. Juliet hadn't turned blue again, and they never found a reason for it, except suggesting that the medicine for pre-eclampsia could have caused it. My blood pressure returned to more normal levels with the medication I had been given.

The day after we got home, Matthieu's aunt Christine stopped over from Peru on her way to France and she was the first one in the extended family to hold Juliet. My mother came the next day, wreathed in smiles at holding her first grandchild. "She's so beautiful," she exclaimed softly with tears in her eyes. She stayed for a week, a reassuring and strengthening presence in my vulnerable state.

The first time I walked with Matthieu to the train stop for his return to work, I felt like I was just playing at being a mom. I was pretending. There was no way this baby could have actually come from me; there was no way she was mine. I was giggling weakly to myself, clutching the stroller for support all the way back to the apartment. There I tried to rein in my terror at being left all alone with her for the first time. My mom had already left the week before.

A few months later, my general physician was surprised to see how low my iron levels were. He talked to my OB-GYN, who later told me I probably should have had a blood transfusion after the birth. But no one had told me anything other than to take some iron, not that I would be weak, not how much iron to take, or for how long.

For those first two months, I was in pure survival mode. I was suffering from a mild form of post-partum depression without realizing it. My OB-GYN and psychiatrist had warned me, working together during my pregnancy to give me comprehensive medical care after all my attempts to go off anti-depressants were unsuccessful. I knew what PPD was, but I didn't consider myself depressed. However, I was acting in strange ways that seemed exaggerated even in my own eyes. When someone gave me a baby gift that was the wrong size, I got really mad.

At night, I got up and brought Juliet with me to the rocker, and after feeding her, set her gently down in the crib. I stepped on the floor lamp to shut it off, and it made two noises. "*Ka*" as I put my foot down, "*click*" as I lifted my foot off again.

One night after having had almost no sleep, Juliet woke up again on the second "*click,*" and I angrily took her in my arms and sat back down in the chair. Suddenly I had an ugly vision of throwing her across the room and watching her go *splat* against the wall. I took a deep breath, unable to let go of the trembling anger but feeling frightened by my thoughts.

I finally understood that this was post-partum depression, and I woke Matthieu up and told him what happened. He took Juliet in his arms and sat down in the chair while I went back to bed. That was the only incident that occurred, but it gave me a clearer understanding of the challenges faced by single moms and those with absent husbands.

After the first two months, things started to get much easier. I made friends with Amanda, who lived across the hall from me and had a newborn son as well. We lived an idyllic life, strolling on the boardwalk along the Hudson River, sitting in cafés, sipping coffee as our babies shook cloth rattlers back and forth before putting them in their mouths. We hit the sales at Baby Gap and brought our babies to music class in Tribeca. It was the perfect introduction to motherhood.

But in August it was time to move. The government grant was over, and the rents were going back up. We decided to look into unfashionable—but cheaper—Staten Island. A free twenty-five minute ferry ride would get Matthieu to his job and me to my old neighborhood to hang out with Amanda.

We discovered an upscale housing project that didn't ask for a cap on salary to participate. We put our name in the hat, and due to our excellent financial situation, were handpicked for a spacious two-bedroom apartment with hardwood floors.

I bought sheer Pottery Barn curtains for our windows and embroidered flowered ones for Juliet's room. I spent lazy days pushing Juliet in the bucket swings at the empty playground. Several times a week, I took the ferry into Lower Manhattan, holding the locked stroller safely in my grip as I sat inside. I stared dreamily at the Statue of Liberty, feeling the breeze on my cheeks as we sped by.

I rocked Juliet in the comfortable brown armchair, placed near the window in the sun. We listened to the gentle noises outside as the breeze lifted the curtains lightly. I was feeding her and rocking, lazily, happily, when suddenly there was a loud noise outside. She latched off and looked at me, startled. I smiled at her and quietly said, "It's okay." She smiled and went back to feeding. The loud noise occurred again, and once again she latched off and looked at me. I smiled and repeated, "It's okay." When the loud noise happened a third time, she didn't latch off, but just turned her eye upwards to meet mine. I smiled reassuringly and mouthed, "It's okay." She smiled and turned back to the business of eating. Those were simple, sweet days when my daughter fit across my belly, a warm bundle in the crook of my arms.

After a few months in Staten Island, we went to Florida for our three-year wedding anniversary. During the day, we took Juliet to the pool with her sunglasses and bonnet, heavily slathered with sunscreen. In the early evening, we went to the beach and watched her smile as the salty breeze blew on her bare limbs. Each night, we ate dinner at the same Cuban restaurant while she slept in the stroller next to us.

One evening, we walked to our usual place for dinner in the waning light, my arm around Matthieu's waist as he pushed the stroller. "You know," he said. "While I was in the shower, I was thinking. If we're going to be living in the suburbs now, we may as well move back to France and live in the suburbs there."

Suddenly, all my strength left me and I said, "Wait. I need to sit down." I took a seat on the low wall that bordered a parking lot and looked up at him.

"Why?" he asked, almost laughing, his forehead wrinkling in confusion. "I'm not saying we need to do it. It's just an idea I had. But we can stay in New York if you'd rather."

"Yes, I know you were just expressing the idea," was my response. "But I also know that God was waiting for you to be ready to move back to France before He brought us there. And now that you're ready, He won't delay in carrying it out."

Sure enough—the small office in Paris had an opening within a month. In two months, we were there.

"I will call them 'my people' who are not my people; and I will call her 'my loved one' who is not my loved one." Romans 9

21

PAUSE BUTTON

I would soon find out that living in Paris as a young, single woman and living in the suburbs, pregnant with a toddler, were two very different beasts.

We launched our international move by staying with Matthieu's parents in their comfortable, worn house for the first two months. They couldn't have been more welcoming, and we even had a little privacy, sleeping in one of the downstairs bedrooms that used to belong to one of his brothers. The small inconvenience of taking a shower in a sectioned-off portion of the garage with an old, dirty shower curtain that clung to your legs was minimal when you balanced it with the uniquely scented Le Petit Marseillais soap and shampoo, whose natural perfumes smelled like a spa.

As soon we could, we rented an apartment in Sceaux (pronounced "so"), a neighboring city known for a huge château with its extensive grounds and park. The Parc de Sceaux was where Matthieu used to run and explore with his classmates as a kid.

We planned on having another baby right away, and unlike the first time, I got pregnant quickly. Juliet was starting to crawl and was no longer happy to accompany me on my coffee-sipping shopping excursions. In any case, there was little chance for that.

The shops in the small town center were closed on Sundays and Mondays, and I wandered around the ghost town with nothing to do. On other weekdays, I pushed Juliet's stroller down the busy street towards the cobblestone pedestrian area with small shops on either side—bakeries, the butcher, vegetable stands, the fishmonger, a few pharmacies, and some small clothing shops. I tried to embrace the French way of shopping at the *marché*, but I couldn't carry it all back, and it was more expensive than going to Monoprix.

The main pedestrian walkway led to a narrow stone cathedral on a shaded street and eventually fed into the magnificent park and château. I pushed the jogging stroller lightly over the stones onto the shady path carpeted with pine needles, but I didn't really have anywhere to go, and I had no one to share it with. This idyllic vision of pushing a stroller through such lovely surroundings and breathing in the air of France was, in fact, quite lonely.

We wasted no time in contacting our sister church in Paris where we started to attend once a week. The first thing I noticed about the church was how small it was. The second was how inferior the singing was compared to our church in New York. Also, although my French was relatively fluent, if I dozed off for just a minute during the sermon, there was no coming back. There was enough of the French culture seeping into the fellowship at church, and I perceived a reserve in them that made me not want to try too hard.

The church was still reeling from the same upset that we had had two years back, but while New York had mostly moved forward in a positive direction, the French church seemed leagues behind in their healing. I found myself looking around during the service each week with my lip curled, thinking, *are we still talking about this church issue? Get over it. What am I doing here? I don't care about you. And I don't care about you*, as I glared at each of them from behind.

I grew resentful because the things that were supposed to be easy and delightful—being married, having babies, living in France—were simply not. I couldn't understand why life was so full of loneliness and challenges in what was supposed to be the golden era of raising a family. I was frustrated that nothing matched up to how I had pictured it. But I swallowed my resentment and seethed quietly because I knew that, in places I had seen with my own eyes, people had no running water and not enough food. There was nothing I could justifiably complain about.

My second pregnancy was almost as difficult as the first, except that I was diagnosed with celiac disease halfway through the pregnancy. Once I reluctantly gave up the baguettes and patisseries, I was sick much less often. Although. . . my weaning off these foods happened more in fits and starts than it did cold turkey as I frequently walked by the buttery smell of croissants baking at the *boulangerie* and weighed temptation against potential stomach upset. Potential upset usually held little sway when confronted with immediate buttery croissants.

Juliet had started to talk, saying her own name as her first word and taking those first tentative steps from the window to the railing of the balcony as her father watched from the other side of the glass. We got several bags of high quality boy clothes from another mom who was done having babies and wanted them out—the clothes, not the babies—and I washed and folded the navy blue onesies in anticipation of our new arrival.

Although the official due date in France was not until forty-one weeks, I expected to deliver at forty weeks because that was the due date in my mind. The morning I hit forty weeks, I woke up with the certainty that my water was leaking as it had in the first pregnancy, and I went to the hospital, fully expecting to be admitted, but they sent me home. I was disappointed and angry as we picked Juliet up at my in-laws and stayed for tea and small talk. I didn't want small talk—I wanted great events.

Nothing out of the ordinary occurred in the week preceding my next appointment, so I went in as planned at forty-one weeks, sure they would admit me even though I still wasn't having any contractions. They did.

As it turned out, my water had leaked at some point during the week, but because I didn't give birth right away, infection set in. I had already been diagnosed with Streptococcus B and knew I would be getting antibiotics during the delivery, but this complicated things because the infection had already started spreading. There was also meconium in the amniotic fluid.

The room I was ushered into was sterile, with ugly fluorescent lights and only medical equipment for decoration. I had slowly gotten used to the fact that medical care in France, albeit excellent, was not geared towards comfort. The tongue depressors were made of plastic that got washed after use, you had to provide your own jars in which to bring urine samples, and the waiting rooms were often stuffy closets with plastic folding chairs and three-year old magazines. This room would have depressed me had I not been so focused on the task at hand.

I was induced immediately and set up for monitoring. Once again, I decided to have the epidural about midway through the afternoon so I could first connect with the labor process. But by the time I was ready, or more accurately—good and panicked—it was hard to insert the needle because the contractions were coming on so strongly.

"Curl up in a ball," the midwife ordered as she put her elbows on my shoulders and pushed my body downwards. I struggled to breathe and comply with my enormous belly getting in the way. The doctor started to insert the needle.

"Stop," I gasped. "I'm having another contraction." They waited until it passed and I was able to get into position again. When he finally got the needle in after half a dozen tries, only half of my body was numb, so I asked the doctor to fix it, getting back into a seated position on the edge of the table. The whole procedure seemed to take hours.

My Gabriel was born at nearly eleven o'clock that night, a full day after I was admitted. During the second half of labor and throughout the pushing, I was shaking with a full-blown fever as the doctors scurried around me adjusting this medicine or checking that monitor. In spite of distractions from the fever and the relief the epidural provided, when the time came to deliver, I found that my nine-pound baby hurt a lot more coming out than my seven-pounder had. I trembled and pushed and shook with fever and strained to get the baby out as quickly as possible, even when it seemed I would not have enough strength left to do so.

He was completely blue. He didn't respond at all as they dangled him upside down and cleaned his airways and tried to get him to breathe. The medical team rushed off with him quickly, leaving me alone with Matthieu. I was still shaking with fever and incognizant of what was happening. I just thought my baby needed a little extra help; it never occurred to me that something might actually be wrong.

Matthieu was trying to reassure me, but he was worried and was offering desperate, silent prayers. After an impossibly long time, he heard a baby cry loudly, and after an even longer time, they came back in and announced that they had resuscitated him, but he would need to stay in the NICU as he was not in good condition. They promised to bring him to me in a short while. I was confused and didn't understand what it all meant. Did he need to be in an incubator? How could they bring him to me if he was not doing well? But I was too tired to ask any questions.

After some time, two midwives walked in with a small bundle and set it on my chest. When I looked down at his little face, I had to hide my dismay. Whereas Juliet's face had been beautiful and delicate right after birth, Gabriel's was reddish blue with large swollen features.

I began to feed him, caressing his head and arms. I looked into his eyes and spoke gently, "Hello, little Gabriel. I'm your mommy, and you're my little prince. I will love you for the rest of my life." I held him and held him, feeding and caressing, until my head started swaying back and forth with fatigue. The midwives just stood around and watched.

Why are they letting me hold him this long? I thought to myself. *This can't be good for him. I thought he had to go to emergency care. Plus I'm so exhausted.*

But the doctors and midwives quietly noticed that his vital signs were improving steadily. It was his mother he needed, more than the medical equipment, more than the intervention. The miracle was staring me in the face, but I could barely open my fatigued eyes to see it. Finally, they took him from me and brought him to the "Kangaroo Room" so he would be near where I slept.

My fever broke. I stopped trembling and felt better almost instantly, and by the time they wheeled me into my room, my heart was filled with joy. *I did it. He's out.* I thought—and because we were only going to have two children—*I will never have to give birth again.*

As sick as I had been during the delivery, I was now feeling great. I had none of the tearing or blood loss I had had with Juliet. I couldn't believe how strong I felt. *So this is what normal post-delivery is supposed to feel like.*

I cried when Juliet came to visit her little brother for the first time. She, who had seemed like such a baby, now looked mammoth in comparison. I watched her giant face next to the clear, plastic bassinet, cooing at Gabriel before leaping up on the bed as I laughed with tears streaming down my face.

I knew our life would be different, but I don't think I was prepared for the hardship of having two children. Gabriel was born in the bitter cold of winter. He had colic and cried constantly. Unlike my strolls with Juliet on the boardwalk in spring, it was too cold to go outside, so I was stuck indoors with a restless toddler and a screaming newborn. I felt like I was losing my mind.

The first time I ventured to bring our double stroller down to the lobby for a walk, everyone bundled against the cold, I had to fold the thing up to fit into our tiny, French elevator. Juliet was on foot and promptly took off as soon as the doors opened; Gabriel was in my arms. I was trying to open the double stroller with just one hand while holding a baby in the other, and I was ready to scream with murderous rage. I envisioned taking a shotgun to the stupid guy who had invented the double stroller and, well…that was as far as I plotted.

This was not a period of peace and reflection; this was survival. Faith and God were nowhere in my picture. I wasn't trying to read the Bible or pray. I wasn't having any spiritual conversations. I wasn't having any conversations that didn't involve, "Juliet, NO," or "Gabriel, I just fed you." I had put a pause button on my faith.

I was waking up sometimes as often as every forty-five minutes to try and soothe Gabriel back to sleep. During the day, I put him in the stroller and rocked him back and forth to ease the colic and the crying, sometimes jerking it harder than necessary.

Oh my son, my son. You didn't deserve this brutal welcome into the world. Why is it the hardest job we'll ever have in our lives must be done on so little sleep when riding wave upon wave of depression, loneliness, and hormonal changes?

By the time spring rolled around, we decided to buy an apartment. After first looking in our own neighborhood, we began to focus on the western suburbs of Paris in the La Défense area. A lot of young couples from our church lived there, and I was starting to open up more in the fellowship. As the weather improved, I was also slowly regaining my sanity and starting to realize how much I needed those relationships.

Matthieu decided to call someone in church who lived in this suburb to see if they knew anything about a particular building we saw that had an affordable apartment for sale. When we described the apartment we were looking at online, he said, "Wait. I think that's Frédéric and Danila's apartment. They just put it on the market. You should give them a call."

I had been interested in getting to know Danila ever since I arrived at church that first day and saw she had a daughter the same age. She also had a second daughter three months before I had Gabriel, and the potential of harmonious play dates between us looked promising.

It seemed fortuitous that the apartment we were looking at should be theirs, especially when we found out they had decided to stay in the city and were taking a larger apartment about a fifteen-minute's walk away. Frédéric proposed we cancel with the agency and come visit the apartment directly, so neither of us had to pay the extra fee; then we could stay and have lunch.

The sun streamed in through the bay windows, which had a view over the city of Puteaux, the Seine, and even the Eiffel Tower in the distance if we craned our heads far enough to the left. The kitchen was a narrow walk-through, and the living room was spacious. There was plenty of room in the children's bedroom for two kids, but the parental bedroom was even bigger and would comfortably hold all our books and CDs, our desk and computer, our bed, and the tall, deep wardrobes that could hide everything else. It was modern, clean, and perfectly located, and the tall building reminded us of living in New York.

That day at Fred and Danila's, we fell into easy conversation as we watched our children play together. It seemed that with our shared faith, proximity, and parallel stage in life, our friendship was destined to grow deeper. This was only the beginning of friendships that sprung up with other mothers in the building and with other friends from church also living within walking distance. Sometimes those two worlds collided in a beautifully organic way.

In retrospect, I have to admit that I never could have planned such a perfect alignment of needs being met and desires being fulfilled. I was set securely in the midst of bosom friends where my children were able to grow in a community, rather than solitude. I realized I may have pushed the pause button on my faith, but God didn't push the pause button on me.

God sets the lonely in families. Psalm 68

22

SMALL CONCERNS

The first thing I did, once I burrowed a path through the ceiling-high boxes in our new apartment, was to make my way over to the mall across the street. We had parked our car there the first time we visited the apartment, and I confess it only added to the attraction of our choice. While I had once been seduced by white stone Parisian buildings and broad tree-lined avenues, I was now lured by an indoor commercial center that boasted both a Starbucks and Toys R' Us.

Our building was the tallest residential tower in Europe, and its residents were from all over the world. There was a *maternelle*—the public pre-school and kindergarten—on the ground floor, so when Juliet started attending at the age of three, I simply took the elevators to the ground floor and jogged down a small flight of stairs. There were mothers in the building with similar aged-children, and we began to get acquainted as we congregated in front of the school.

My particular friends were Faisa from Algeria, Zali from Mayotte, and Amina, whose family was Moroccan. We all lived in the same building with Zali right next door, and we each had children entering school the same year. We created our own habits, meeting constantly in each other's apartments for the afternoon snack, or borrowing cups of sugar or pots of Nutella if the need arose. If I heard a knock on the door when there were brownies in the oven, I laughed. "Oh that must be Zali, here to collect."

When we first arrived at the end of summer, Gabriel was only eight months old and Juliet was just over two, so I gratefully spent a lot of that first winter in the mall across the street, hiding from the horrific weather in the comfort of cheerfully lit stores. The financial district was outside the mall, headed by the Grand Arche de La Défense, the huge white arc set upon an immense staircase, which paralleled the more famous Arc de Triomphe in the distance. Tall office buildings lined the wide esplanade where businessmen and women walked in groups or talked on the phone. As our children got older, they wove their bikes back and forth down the broad pavement or sat on the edge of the fountain on hot days, plunging their feet into the icy water.

The first time I spoke to Amina was when we crossed paths at Toys R'Us and recognized each other from the few brief meetings at the playground. I knew she had just given birth, and I asked about her baby girl. Her eyes filled with tears as she told me that her daughter was in the hospital with pneumonia. The hospital had sent her home several times, dismissing her baby's condition as nothing more than a cold. When she finally got desperate enough to bring her in again one night, she was told that if she had waited until morning, her daughter would be dead.

"Is there anything I can do to help?" I asked, my own eyes filling with tears. "I can make dinner and bring it over, or I can do your laundry for you."

"No, no—thank you. It's alright," she answered with a watery smile. When I got to know her better, I guessed that perhaps she didn't want me to see how small their apartment was or have to explain that they only ate *halal*. This was the Muslim ritual of sacrificing animals with a prayer, and it was the only meat Muslims could eat. It wasn't long before we were such good friends I bought *halal* from time to time and kept it in the freezer for when they dropped by for lunch.

We couldn't have been more different on the outside—Amina was twelve years younger, we had different religions, different cultures and languages—and yet we had kindred spirits. We met at the playground or in the mall, cracking jokes and making fun of life and ourselves.

After the isolation of Sceaux, this happy communion of souls and stores was bliss.

A casual friend from church named Isabelle was getting married to Olivier and moving in around the corner from us. We were invited to the wedding, and I watched her walk down the aisle in a tiny stone church, tucked away in Bièvres. This city reminded me of Westchester County in New York with the autumn foliage and the old houses.

Matthieu and I had dropped the kids off at their grandparents, so we were early for the ceremony. We stopped off in a little wooden café where we sipped cappuccinos and talked intimately with our hands intertwined. The modest ceremony led to a grand dinner with candlelit tables set in a converted barn with high ceiling rafters. I felt giddy as Matthieu twirled me around the dance floor, and I smiled at various faces in the warm glow of lights, thinking, *I care about you. And I care about you too. It's different now.* I was accepting my new culture, my new church, and my new life.

Amina already had three children, her eldest a day younger than Juliet. I don't know if it was their family that prompted me, or if it was just the most basic desire that could not be stifled, but I started thinking about having another child. I struggled with guilt when I thought about the need for adoption, the overpopulated world, and every other valid reason for not having more children. In spite of everything, all I could think about was watching my belly expand with life again, breathing in my newborn's scent, and breastfeeding.

So we had our third baby, grown in the same nauseous state as each of my babies. I threw up the full nine months as I had done with Juliet, even with the gluten-free diet. I had plumped up again with my antidepressants, poor eating habits, and hectic schedule. But by the time my baby was ready to be born, I was actually four pounds less than I had been before I got pregnant. Pregnancy would be a perfect way to diet if it were not sure to be followed by chocolate-laced sleeplessness.

The months passed in the usual way with quiet throwing up in the tiny bathroom papered in green Japanese wallpaper, while a raucous four-year old birthday party was carrying on in the living room. I succumbed to the delicious call of the cool sheets as I took naps along with the children. I floated lazily through the flurry of activities centered on small children. Through it all, this pregnancy felt different than the other two. I knew to expect the discomfort, but I also knew to expect the joy. In addition, Amina was also pregnant with her fourth child, and we shared this bond along with the laughter and friendship.

On a day when my belly was growing heavy, and I was sitting with my feet on Amina's lap, enjoying her and Faisa's company while Matthieu was away traveling, the doorbell rang. I heaved myself up to answer it and at the door was Prisca, along with a group of friends from church who had organized a surprise baby shower with my friends from the building. Everyone laughed at my stunned reaction and pushed their way in, setting up food and gifts. Then we were eating, and I was opening gifts. We played games, and they each shared what they loved about me. It was the opposite of all alone.

I was nearing the end of my pregnancy in the fall. Forty weeks passed. Forty-one weeks passed, and my baby didn't show any signs of coming out.

"You're baby is measuring over eleven pounds," the midwife said at my forty-one week visit.

"What?" I exclaimed in disbelief. "Then I'll have to have a C-section."

"Well, it's hard to say," she continued. "You also have more than the usual amount of amniotic fluid, and I think that's why nothing's happening. He's not able to push on your cervix to start the contractions because there's too much fluid in the way."

Finally, she said, "Come in next week if you haven't started your labor process before then, and we'll have to induce you."

At forty-two weeks, I went in first thing in the morning with my suitcase full of baby pajamas and I was brought into another ugly, sterile room. I expected them to hook me up to an IV right away to induce labor, but all they did was insert something to cause contractions and send me up to my hospital room to wait for it to work.

Matthieu accompanied me to my hospital room where we spent the day cozily flipping through the book of baby names as we had a sudden panic that maybe we hadn't chosen the right one. A woman came in and lay on the other bed, sucking in her breath and hissing it out as her contractions came and went. They quickly whisked her off to the delivery rooms within the hour. Evening fell, and there had been no contractions—nary a squeeze to disturb my comfort. So Matthieu left me to go home.

In the morning, the midwives said we were going to have to induce labor more forcefully through an injection, but it didn't work. By the end of the afternoon, the intern was trying to figure out what to do with me. She talked about breaking my water as a way of inducing, or perhaps just going straight for the C-section. She said she would talk to the doctor and see what the next step would be.

Finally she said, "Why don't you go upstairs, take a shower, eat some dinner, and then come back down and we'll figure out what to do."

Matthieu assisted me as I wrapped my hospital gown around me. There was no moving pole available to attach the IV, so the nurse told me I'd have to carry it. We exited into the central corridor of the hospital, where visitors were rushing back and forth in winter coats, the cold air whipping in with them. I pulled my thin hospital gown more securely around me and shuffled forward in my slippers and bare legs.

Matthieu took the IV bag from me and held me by the arm in a protective gesture as we made our way over to the elevator. I was starting to feel contractions just from walking. Although they were bearable, they did give me the vulnerable impression that my baby could pop out of my body any second, as if there was nothing to keep the baby in but a thin membrane, and meanwhile there was a relentless pressure that threatened to break it.

The elevator was the usual tiny French style that fit just two of us with no room to spare.

"Just watch," Matthieu said with a wicked grin. "You're gonna lose your water and short-circuit the elevator. Then you'll have to give birth standing up."

I was leaning with one hand on the elevator panel as the pressure bore down, the other hand under my belly trying to hold everything in, and I giggled pathetically. "Don't make me laugh."

When we got to the public bathroom, and I realized I couldn't even take my hospital gown off because of the IV, it was the final straw. I burst into bitter tears. "There's not even a shelf for me to put the soap.

How am I supposed to bend down in this state to pick up the soap?" I sobbed.

Matthieu was there comforting me, holding my gown for me, which was still attached to the IV, and holding the soap dish up high for me so I could reach it. Finally I was clean, fed, and calm, and we made our way back downstairs.

By the time we returned, the midwives confirmed that my contractions had started in earnest.

"Let's get you your epidural, and then we're going to break the water," the new midwife said.

The epidural worked right away. Within a half-hour, my contractions were coming quickly and with such intensity I couldn't talk because of the pain, even with the epidural. This had never happened to me before. I hesitantly told the intern about it, assuming I would just have to bear it, but she said they would have the anesthesiologist come back.

Having needed twelve hours to give birth after being induced in both prior pregnancies, I settled down to wait the night. But in just another half-hour, the intern, who had been monitoring my progress from her station, came in and chirped, "It's time to give birth."

I was shocked. "But...but I'm not ready. I can't feel anything." More than that, I was not emotionally ready. I thought I would have hours to mentally prepare myself.

"Nope. It's right now," she sang out cheerfully. It wasn't even midnight.

Once I got into the rhythm of pushing, the birth was quick, painless and perfect. Matthieu got to cut the cord for the first time, and I got to hold my baby straight out of the womb, feeling all the joy and wonder, instead of feeling like I was going to fall asleep on top of him. Every ounce of me was aware of the divine blessings that had showered down on me as I held my third healthy baby—my William.

I don't remember those early months, mainly because they were so peaceful. Gabriel had been given a part-time spot in the highly coveted *crèche*, the nursery across the street where he stacked cubes in bright yellow rooms and cooed with joy when I came to pick him up. Mornings were a simple routine of going down the stairs to bring Juliet to *maternelle*, then walking across the street to bring Gabriel to the *crèche* with William in his stroller. I then met up with Amina and her baby, and together we walked over to Starbucks where everyone knew us by name. We sauntered through the various stores, looking for good deals, and made plans for our lives in a happy, caffeinated glow.

Matthieu and I squeezed the extra baby-seat into our tiny car as we headed off for church in Paris each Sunday. I usually found myself praying, "Thank you God that we're all together as a family. Thank you that we're going to church on a Sunday morning and that I'm not drunk somewhere or spending the day alone in some dark room with a hangover. I love the life you gave me."

Then on the weekdays after school, I sat in the park with the other moms, watching our children play—Amina, Faisa, Zali and I—our sandals kicked off as a sunny breeze filtered by. Sometimes I brought coffee in a thermos and some cookies I had baked, and the other moms congregated around us, laughing at my funny non-French ways and reaping their benefits.

The days passed us by in a fog of baby fatigue, young children clamoring with needs, friendship, and peace among ourselves, a sort of contentment mixed with survival, borne by tears and laughter—a time reserved for the mothers of young families with simple needs, not experienced in my life before or since.

Write on them all the words of this law when you have crossed over to enter the land the Lord your God is giving you, a land flowing with milk and honey, just as the Lord, the God of your ancestors, promised you. Deuteronomy 27

23

THE GARDEN OF EDEN

Matthieu's grandparents had a house made of black lava stone in Auvergne where he spent most of his summers. There were twenty rooms, six bedrooms spread over a few floors, and the rooms in the house were decorated according to period—Louis XV1, Napoleon, etc. There was a winery, aviaries and stables, a barn, and a vast garden with acres of orchards, wooded areas, and fountains fed by the property's own spring.

Matthieu ate simple lunches with his grandparents at the massive table in the kitchen, formed from one thick wooden slab. They always ate the same thing—hearty *Poilâne* bread, sweet crispy apples from the orchard, and *Saint Nectaire* cheese, cut from a large wheel stored in the basement. At night, he sat peacefully with his grandparents, listening to the occasional *vroom* as a car passed by, the crackle of magnolia leaves in the fire, and the *toc, toc, toc* of the large grandfather clock on the wall. To Matthieu, having a home and garden with such simple pleasures as he had experienced at his grandparents' house was the crowning touch to a complete life made happy by God and family.

I was less drawn to the idea of settling down, but I did assume that owning a house was something that would eventually come to pass. Yet, from the time I left home at the age of eighteen, the idea never held any romance for me. I didn't like the thought of being tied down to one place. Apart from the occasional musing—*a big old stone house in the countryside of France would be really magical*—it always fell lower in priority than the convenience of living in a metropolitan area.

But there came a time when our apartment started to feel small, even to me. We could comfortably fit the crib in our large bedroom, and the children slept in bunk beds in theirs, but I knew this would not be a long-term solution. I, who had long been attracted to a bohemian lifestyle, started to long for a place where we could just open the back door and send the children out to play without it becoming a family production.

Suddenly our desires and life's circumstances were aligned, and together we focused on the idea of buying a house. Without praying directly about it, we expressed a wish list to each other when talking about our dream house. "In Peru, a lot of houses have tall stone walls, and the rooms of the house border the walls on the inside of the property," Matthieu reminisced. "When they close the gates at the end of the day, they have an interior courtyard that's completely hidden from view. I think that would be a really cool thing to have."

"I know this is silly," I said one day, "but I think it would be nice to have a vegetable garden where we could grow our own vegetables, and even have a well—that way we could be completely self-sufficient." I smiled at my longing; it was really just a pipe dream if we weren't planning on moving to the country. We both hoped for a good school system, but as for the rest of the details, we just figured it would all work out somehow.

We had started working with an agent, and one day he called and said he had the perfect house for us in a suburb we hadn't even considered because it was out of our price range. We knew this offer must be too good to be true because the houses in that area started at half a million. We tried to find the house online, sure there was a major flaw —maybe it was attached to a car dealership or something. In fact, we were so certain it would be a dump we came close to canceling the appointment. But we had nothing else to do, so we went.

When we arrived at the address, we were convinced it had to be the wrong one. This was too nice of a neighborhood for the price of the house he had quoted. But no. There was the agent, waving to us and directing us to a nearby parking space.

He rang the doorbell as I looked around in admiration at all the quaint houses, the blue sky, and the wide quiet street with a cycling path. When the owners opened the gates to welcome us, the first thing I saw was the purple flowering plum tree shading the patio by the front door and the green grass on the side lawn with cheerful flowers planted everywhere.

Just like the Garden of Eden, I thought. After living in New York City, a desert, and a high-rise apartment in La Défense, we found ourselves *here*—in a small garden with low, fruit-bearing trees, green grass, bursts of colorful flowers, and a rose bush over the well. A well that worked.

Before we knew it, we were being led to the second part of the property, hidden behind the fence and bushes that contained the vegetable garden. This triangular bit of land was enclosed with tall, green laurel hedges, and the owner had turned the rich brown earth in preparation for planting season. "The soil here is very rich," he told us. "Everything grows well, except leeks. The soil is too sandy."

He pointed to the only plants that were visible in three of the raised rows. "Do you know what kind of potatoes those are?" he asked me. I shook my head with a smile. I had never even seen a potato plant before and had trouble associating the green leaves with those starchy vegetables.

"Think of Gainsburg's daughter," he hinted, referencing the famous French singer whose daughter was a well-known actress.

"Charlotte," I exclaimed with a laugh. He winked at me as he reached for a pitchfork and started digging underneath the roots of the plant. Reddish potatoes were uncovered as they lay nestled in the brown earth, and he pulled one out to show me. The children were talking to the owner's wife in chirping, excited voices that made her smile.

The cement terrace at the back of the house was shaded by a massive linden tree and was bordered on one side by a studio and chicken coop, on another side by an apricot tree, and on the third, by a row of bay laurels. This gave the house the enclosed courtyard that

Matthieu had wished for. As we went inside to visit the rooms, the agent told us the public schools were excellent.

To our amazement, it was looking like even our unformed prayers, our secret desires, were being answered. As it was, the house was too small for our family of five, and we wouldn't have the money for renovations with the increased mortgage payments. Still, we knew we had found the right place to live, and we made an offer instantly.

In the three months between signing the purchase promise and signing the deed, we started to take a look at the work that needed to be done. We figured we could temporarily make do with the small space if we had to. At least we were in the right location with the right schools, and it had a big garden. Matthieu's parents offered to lend us some money so we could hire someone to do the masonry, and we found a company cheap enough to build the stairwell and extra bedrooms we needed.

At the beginning of July right after school finished, we went to Brittany for two weeks. We rented a house there each summer with our extended family, and I had come to love this region. The salty sea air, the cold bracing winds, the craggy cliffs…Brittany was so wild and savage it shook me out of my winter lethargy and filled my nostrils with life. The cousins had formed tight bonds from a young age, and they played together loudly. We ate leisurely meals in the shade outdoors, the plates balanced on three plastic tables that were shoved together. On Bastille Day each year, we all trooped down to the beach at night to watch the fireworks.

That summer we could barely enjoy our time there because our hearts were on our new home, and our minds on everything the move entailed. Then Matthieu's cherished aunt Christine died. We knew it was coming; she had gotten skin cancer from living in high altitudes in the mountains of Peru. Her dream was always to die in Cusco where she had spent her whole life since girlhood. She rented a bedroom in the tiny cupola of a house because she wanted to give as much of her income as possible to the poor. She taught computers at the university and started an association to help housemaids, who had been taken from their parents with the promise of a better life in the city, but who were treated like slaves. The entire city of Cusco knew this Christine who put her heart, her funds, and her hands towards anything and anyone in need.

She came back to France just two weeks before her death, still hoping she would be able to return to her home to die among her people—those she had lived with and loved her whole life—but it was soon clear she would not be able to go back. Matthieu and I went with the kids to see her right before leaving for Brittany—she who had been the first family member to hold Juliet after she was born. Christine smiled gently as she always did. She seemed strong enough and in good spirits as she packed her bags for her trip to Grenoble to see her older sister.

But in Grenoble, within days, she was reduced to a wheelchair and unable to speak; from there, she quickly fell into a coma. Halfway through our stay in Brittany, Matthieu's father rushed into the room, breathless. *"Christine est morte."*

Her breathing had grown quieter in her coma. Her brother-in-law saw the end coming and put a mirror under her nose to see if she was still breathing. This was how he knew that in the moment she drew her last breath—letting it out with a long sigh—that the bells of the village church suddenly started ringing clearly and joyfully. As her spirit left her body, the clanging bells pealed in jubilant celebration. Astonished, her brother-in-law inquired why the bells had tolled at that precise moment and learned there had just been a baptism.

This dear Aunt Christine left us money from her inheritance—her portion of the family heritage, of which she used nothing for her own needs. With this gift, along with the loan from Matthieu's parents, we were able to renovate our tiny house into something more suited to a family of five.

It's strange how sometimes life's heartaches come at the same time as life's blessings. Two weeks held two events, with Matthieu weeping as he dropped a handful of earth on his beloved Christine's tomb and us waving at the gate of our new house as the previous owners drove away, before turning and grinning at each other in excitement at the new adventure before us.

It was heartache, it was joy—and we were alive.

If you falter in the time of trouble, how small is your strength? Proverbs 24

24

A SURPRISE GIFT

After a trying year of construction, I cautiously entered a new season—I would no longer be a mother to small babies for the first time in seven years. William, though only two, was to enter public pre-school, and there was a mad, and unsuccessful, rush to get him potty trained. I also decided that in addition to teaching private English classes, this would be the year to reclaim my life and my figure. I signed up for yoga.

I still harbored a deep, intense longing to have another baby, but I forced myself to look to the future. I had already been blessed with three beautiful children, I was forty-two years old, and we could barely afford the plane tickets to the States as it was.

"You can have grandchildren next," said Matthieu, who suffered no such longing.

But then one month my period was late. Matthieu was in London on business, so he knew nothing about it. The lady at the pharmacy started to explain to me how the test should be done, and I smiled weakly as I told her, "I know the drill." I wanted to rush home and take the test before experiencing the crushing disappointment of the period I was sure would arrive. Instead, the test was positive.

I sat down, trembling with excitement. For just a moment, only

God and I knew this secret, that I was not one being, but two. I walked around that day with this full, knowing, rich feeling—the newness of a life being knit together before the haggard appearance of morning sickness would arrive and cloak everything in somber gray and deeply etched wrinkles.

Of course I told Matthieu over the phone that evening. I couldn't wait until he came home. He was stunned, but very pleased. I felt like God had listened to the deep secret, unreasonable desire of mine to have another baby, saying, "My child, I am far greater than reason. My will is not limited by circumstances."

This time around, in addition to the morning sickness, there was this lack of courage that I had never before experienced. What if I wasn't able to be a good mom—if having four children was too much for me? What if I didn't lose the extra weight this time and fell into ill health, dying early and leaving my kids orphans? As it was, I would be sixty-three years old when my baby turned twenty. That just seemed insanely old to me.

When I hit the twelve-week mark and went in for the standard nuchal fold test for Down's Syndrome, the fluid around the neck measured a little on the thick side. I tried not to worry too much about it and was reassured by friends whose baby's test had also measured thick, only to have the baby turn out absolutely fine. Still, I read up on Down's Syndrome and considered doing a CVS test, similar to an amniocentesis, just to prepare myself for all eventualities.

When reading the Bible one morning, I stumbled upon a scripture that I didn't remember seeing before. It was Exodus 23:26. *I will take away sickness from among you, and none will miscarry or be barren in your land. I will give you a full life span.*

Suddenly, I was filled with hope. God was showing me this scripture *now* to encourage me. He would keep both my baby and me healthy. We would be just fine. As if to reassure me, a week later at the preliminary ultrasound, I saw my baby kicking energetically and sucking his thumb on the large screen.

I rubbed my belly and smiled. *Don't worry, baby. I don't care if there's something wrong. I will love you forever.*

I spoke out loud. "I don't suppose you can tell this early what we're having?"

"With him I can," the doctor answered, not looking away from the screen. "It's a boy."

I curbed the tiny twinge of disappointment I felt at not being able to have a perfectly balanced family with two boys and two girls and figured it was possible for doctors to make mistakes this early.

In the end, I decided to forego the CVS test and trust—to enjoy this last pregnancy I was going to have. I didn't really care what happened; I was sure I would be able to face it with courage. The rocky hormones of the first trimester had started to subside, and even my nausea was starting to abate, which had never happened this early in any of my pregnancies.

The morning after Christmas, I thought about going for a walk since the nausea was completely gone. But when I went to the bathroom, I was surprised, and a little afraid, to see blood. I came out of the bathroom and calmly told Matthieu we needed to go to the emergency room. Even though it was probably nothing that a little bed rest wouldn't cure, we would have to make sure the baby was okay.

We dropped the kids off at my brother-in law's apartment and waited in the Maternity ER before being called in. After having all the questions asked, the routine exams performed, and the reassurance that the cervix was nice and tight, we went for the sonogram. The baby in my womb was still.

Come on little guy, I prodded internally. *We're here to see you. Wake up*, I thought if I nudged the belly with my hand and urged him with my heart, he would wake up.

Matthieu looked worried, but I was sure it was nothing. I looked from him to the intern, who was examining the screen intently without saying anything. But that barely registered with me. *It's fine. Everything's fine*, I thought as I rubbed my belly.

"I can't see any cardiac activity," the intern finally said.

I didn't understand the implications of what she was saying. "Can you check the heartbeat with the sound system?" When she turned the machine on there was just a roar—nothing.

Matthieu was shaking his head sadly, rubbing my arm. The intern spoke. "I'm afraid you've lost the baby."

But I didn't believe it. "Can the heartbeat be hidden? I've heard of that happening."

"Not at fifteen weeks," she answered firmly. "The baby's too big for that to be the case."

I started to feel cold and nauseous as she called in another doctor who confirmed her diagnosis. The pregnancy had ended. "Alright," she said briskly. "We're going to schedule you for a D&C under general anesthesia because the pregnancy is too advanced for your body to do it on its own." She went on to explain the procedure, but I tuned her out as I lay exposed on the table.

We trudged up the five flights of stairs to my brother-in-law's apartment where he and his wife hugged us. Then we turned to face the children, who were watching us with worried expressions. Gabriel was panicked to see me crying and immediately started to cry himself before Matthieu could give the news. Juliet chattered on and on, rapidly trying to process her feelings through words. "So did you really cry? With tears?" William chased the cat.

We went home after that, and I sat on the couch, my chest buckling under the oppression. I tried to process the emptiness that wouldn't be filled with a soft downy head, a tiny baby in my arms, a fourth child to complete this family of ours. I had no idea how to fill the emptiness. I kept waiting to get a phone call from the hospital saying that the equipment was, in fact, not functioning properly and that I should come back in to double check.

That night, I woke up at nearly one o'clock in the morning with cramps that kept me awake for two hours. I began to think I might have to call the hospital in the morning to tell them I wouldn't be able to wait to have the operation. I put on protection despite the fact there wasn't much bleeding and went back to bed.

Then at three o'clock I felt it, the first warm rush of blood. "Honey, I'm bleeding," I said urgently, waking Matthieu up. "We need to go to the hospital."

I got up, leaving a trail on the floor all the way to the bathroom.

After standing indecisively for a moment, Matthieu directed me into the shower, and that's when I felt the first mass being expelled.

I had no choice but to pull on it, and when it fell to the shower floor, I saw it was my baby surrounded by a bloody mass. I saw the small head, the little gray back and tiny butt, and the impossibly tiny foot sticking out from the rest of the matter. "Get me a bag," I ordered numbly. "I have to bring this to the hospital."

Then I felt another mass start to exit, accompanied by a stream of blood. When the room went white, I got down on my hands and knees and put my head against the cool floor outside the shower. I added this to the bag.

I got back up, put heavy protection and sweat pants on, and had Matthieu wake the children while I lay down. We had no choice but to take them with us; surprisingly they were full of courage and in a good mood. Matthieu dressed them and brought them out in the frigid night air to put them in the car.

Meanwhile, I got up from where I had been lying on the bed and felt more matter leaving me, so I went back into the bathroom shower, which is where Matthieu found me. "How am I going to make it out to the car bleeding this much?" I wondered out loud.

But then I thought, *I can't leave my kids sitting out there in the cold and dark all by themselves. I have to get up and go.* So I cleaned up what I could and changed my clothes again.

I was a little faint, so I stretched the seat in the car to lean back, and felt more material coming out of me as we started on our way. There was nothing I could do about it, and the ambiance was strangely festive as the children chattered excitedly.

When we finally arrived at the hospital, they brought a wheelchair and accompanied us down to the Maternity ER. For once, the waiting room was empty, and they were able to see me right away.

Matthieu and the kids stayed in the waiting room while I went to the same uncomfortable half-table I had been on earlier that day. As soon as I stripped, there was another gush of blood and matter. The midwife hurried me on to the table, and as she unsuccessfully tried to staunch the flow, she said, "Relax. Relax. If you keep closing up, I'm not going to be able to stop the bleeding."

I yelled back at her, "If you want me to relax, stop yelling at me." I didn't understand why she couldn't go more slowly and stop jabbing things into me.

She finally saw that the placenta was still partially attached, thus the continual flow of blood. She was ordering the somewhat harried nurse to give her better light, get her pinchers with some grip and hold the basin.

I had to cough while she pulled at the placenta. This was uncomfortable, and I began to miss the general anesthesia I was supposed to have had with the D&C. It went on for a session of about ten minutes of coughing and resting before the speculum came out and she stated she believed she had gotten it all. The ultrasound showed there were still clots in the womb, but she thought the body would take care of that by itself.

They got me cleaned up and on a stretcher out in the hallway. They weren't going to bring me to a room since I wasn't giving birth; they couldn't leave me in the admissions area, yet I still needed to be under surveillance.

My cheeks felt bloodless, and I was nauseous and hot. Everything looked white in the dark corridor. As the nurse was putting the IV in, I closed my eyes gratefully until she slapped my arm to wake me. "Stay with me here."

After fifteen minutes of receiving a glucose solution, plus another medication, I started to feel alive again. I was freezing, and the corridor was drafty, so I asked her to bring me something warmer than a sheet. The nurse was huffing and puffing as she cleaned the room and bagged my things, which she brought to me in a garbage bag. They would all need to be thrown away. I overheard her describing to another nurse how the blood was everywhere—on the floor, the curtains, the walls. The midwife who had treated me came to check up on me. She explained gently that I had hemorrhaged.

I dozed in the corridor, grateful for my warm blankets, grateful the worst was over, grateful my baby had come out on its own and that I wouldn't need an operation. It was about five a.m. and I needed to stay until nine so they could survey the bleeding and decide whether or not I would still need surgery. Matthieu would bring the kids home to sleep and then take them to the play center for the day. The kids were troopers, even on little sleep.

At seven, the moms started coming in—the ones in labor, the ones who thought they were in labor, the ones who were scheduled to be induced or have C-sections that day. I remembered. That was me at one time.

I heard the panting and labored breathing, the excited fathers, the galloping heart rates as they monitored the babies, even an infant's loud, angry cry just before nine.

I lay there as they walked by and ignored me.

Surprisingly, I wasn't as upset as I would have expected to be. Part of what had oppressed me the day before was the idea of an invasion, the thought of going in after my baby and vacuuming him out limb by limb. They wouldn't even be able to tell me if it was a boy or girl, so how could I find a name? I wanted to ask them to check for the heart rate one last time before they operated, but I wasn't sure they would do it. I wasn't sure I would have the courage to ask either.

This way, I felt like my baby made his own choice. We didn't violate the place where he was supposed to be safe. I felt like he was telling me, "I'm done mom. I'm going. You can let go too."

I tried to gather all the positive thoughts, like how I still had my three children, which was no small gift. I tried to think about how we could all go back to the plans we had before—to start doing activities that were only possible with children who were getting older. I could think about what I wanted for my own life. But truthfully, everything paled next to a downy head, tiny fingers, sweet soft breath, a new life in the family. The emptiness was oppressive.

Matthieu handled everything bravely that night—the blood, and caring for the children in the middle of the night. His only concern was that I would be okay. As he pulled out of the emergency drop-off area with the kids, in pitch black at four in the morning, he took the bumpy ramp towards the gate to exit the hospital.

"Man," he said quietly. "These speed bumps are a bit excessive," as the car went bumpity-bump, clatter-bang over them.

Then he realized he was driving his minivan down the *stairs* instead of the ramp.

He wasn't able to back up either. He finally gunned it, and the car went bumpity-bump-clatter-bang all the way back to the top. He sat there breathing hard for a minute, then turned back to the kids and shook his head, exclaiming, "*Quel idiot. Mais, quel idiot!*" What an idiot I am.

This made all the kids laugh and cry out, "*Quel idiot, Papa! Quel idiot!*"

The next day as I was about to leave the hospital, I passed what I thought was the last of the scary blood clots as soon as I stood up. The doctors warned me to watch for dizziness and to take all the medicine and iron they gave me. Then I went home and lay on the couch, noticing with surprise that I felt relatively well. I knew that as long as I could stay on my couch under the blankets I was safe from the worst of the pain.

But grief was crouching in the shadows, waiting for its chance. Earlier that night when the procedure was nearly complete, I asked the midwife to do what I had lacked the courage to do—look at the baby and tell me whether it was the boy that had been predicted, or whether it was a girl. She opened the fold of the towel to see. Then she dumped his body in the garbage.

My baby was a boy. His name is Alistair.

For men are not cast off by the Lord forever. Though he brings grief, he will show compassion, so great is his unfailing love. For he does not willingly bring affliction or grief to the children of men. Lamentations 3

25

BLEEDING

The first time I left the house after the miscarriage was to attend a New Year's Eve dinner with friends. I went reluctantly, hating to leave the warm embrace of my sofa blankets. As we approached their busy suburb, Matthieu prayed, as he always did about everything from the great to the mundane, "God, I pray you give us a great parking spot right in front of their apartment—in Jesus' name, Amen."

I was used to those prayers and to God's faithfulness, but this time, I turned my face away and looked out the window. "Yeah right," I muttered to myself bitterly. "Like *He* answers prayers." Someone pulled out in front of us, leaving a parking spot next to their apartment.

We didn't stay until midnight because it was more than I could handle. I was angry and spoke with a hard edge whenever people talked to me. But when Isabelle sat down on the arm of the sofa and started rubbing my back without saying anything, my tears dripped silently.

I had my grief to deal with, but I was also angry with God for what He had done. I felt like He betrayed me by revealing a scripture about not miscarrying, only then to take my baby away. I had been so sure that God was showing this to me as a promise, to help me face my fears of having a fourth baby. Losing the baby was enough of a shock, but I felt doubly bitter. It was as if He had taunted me with a promise of what could be, before whisking it away.

In addition to our grief over Alistair, there were simultaneous worries that William had hearing problems and my husband had skin cancer. Two days after I lost the baby, Matthieu's doctor said he would need a biopsy for the suspicious mole on his temple. If I had any courage left, it was sucked away by this pronouncement. I was sure he would be dead within the year and that I would be widowed, grieving both my lost baby and my husband.

As ordered by the hospital, I made an appointment with my regular gynecologist, who sent me to get an ultrasound. The technician had just seen me a couple weeks earlier, so she was surprised to see me back, and sorry to learn the news. When she began examining the screen, she twisted her mouth with a "Hm."

Curious, I asked her what was going on, and she explained, "I don't think your body got rid of everything. Look here. See this part? All these colors here? That means there are many open blood vessels, and this part here looks like a piece of the umbilical cord."

My doctor examined the X-ray and agreed with the diagnosis. She told me she'd like to avoid surgery by having me try a medicine which caused contractions. She told me to choose an afternoon when I didn't need to leave the house because there might be a somewhat violent reaction to the medicine. Within an hour of inserting it, I found this indeed to be the case. My heart was beating fast as I experienced a direct reminder of what miscarriage felt like. After some time, however, it slowed down and I went to sleep.

Family life was tumultuous in those days. We needed to hold William down twice a day and spray salt water up his nose to remove the fluid that was blocking his hearing, thereby avoiding surgery. Matthieu had the suspected mole removed in a highly unpleasant procedure, hearing the loud whirring of the saw, feeling his skin tugged and cut, and seeing blood drip off his face. And the children were still talking about the emergency trip to the hospital in the middle of the night.

When Matthieu arrived home from the hospital, he was barely

conscious of his movements as he put the kids to bed. But one look at the bathroom garbage can full of blood penetrated his dull senses. He thought, "I'd better really look around at everything and make sure there's nothing here tomorrow morning that will shock the children."

So, at five o'clock in the morning, he meticulously cleaned the floors, my clothes, the shower, the garbage can, the walls. However, he merely tossed the duvet cover over the sheets until he could have a chance to wash them the next day. Of course the first thing the kids did in the morning was jump on our bed and uncover the huge stain.

A week or two after Matthieu's surgery, we got mixed news. First, the results of Matthieu's biopsy revealed that everything was normal. This made me giddy with relief. Then I had another ultrasound, which revealed more open blood vessels. The doctor proposed trying the same medicine again, but this time, to take it two days in a row to provoke stronger contractions. She thought we had come this far without surgery, and it was such a shame to have to end that way. Surely it must be possible to resolve the matter naturally. I agreed with her.

That night after the treatment, I started hemorrhaging again, and this time it didn't stop. Friends came over to watch the children, and we rushed back to the hospital. The intern took one look, and said, "That's normal bleeding. I'm not sure what you're doing here." Then, as if on cue, I started hemorrhaging again. She called the doctor in charge to see about getting me into surgery right away. But the doctor looked at the ultrasound and the bleeding, which had calmed down again, and vetoed the idea. "No, this time you're good," she said. "Your body has done the trick. There's nothing left." We went home.

I had only taken two weeks to grieve the loss of my baby before giving English lessons again. I opened my home back up for my students, but my heart wasn't in it. I continued to bring my children to their dance and music lessons, and soccer games. I talked to anyone who would listen about my loss, but I was bewildered. I felt I should be able to move on quickly because it was just a miscarriage. Or maybe I felt like God expected me to move on quickly. After all, He was the one who took my baby away.

My own doctor was thorough and kept sending me for ultrasounds until the technician gave a clean bill of health. But the next ultrasound revealed there were just as many open blood vessels as before. So it became evident that I couldn't avoid surgery. By this point, I didn't want to avoid it anymore and was desolate when we fixed a date, and I canceled everything to be there, only to be told the night before that they were overbooked and it would have to be pushed back a week.

By now, I wasn't crying or grieving anymore, at least not in a way I recognized. I was just mad. I was angry that God had betrayed me by promising something He didn't deliver. I was mad that God abandoned me, allowing me all these complications and family worries after such a devastating and traumatic loss. I was mad at people for not knowing how to support me in the way I needed, and it just made me want to isolate myself from everyone. Each time I talked about how ridiculously complicated the healing process had been, I gave a bitter laugh.

The day for my surgery finally arrived. We got there at seven in the morning, and I had to be *à jeun*—fasting since the night before—and pre-scrubbed with an antiseptic soap. The hospital gowns were a flattering dark blue instead of faded white, and I was surprised at how much that simple thing lifted my spirits. As I was lying on the hospital bed with Matthieu sitting at my feet, I was suddenly overwhelmed with joy and gratitude.

I looked at him and grinned. "I feel really happy. I don't have to worry about anyone else—I can just get my own needs taken care of and have the entire day to myself."

He rubbed my feet, his forehead wrinkling in concern. "That's so sad—you're in the *hospital*."

"I know," I said, laughing with sheepish delight.

By about one o'clock my patience was being stretched as my stomach gurgled, and my throat was parched. But even the delay was not enough to shake my good mood. I told Matthieu how happy I was finally to have closure and that later we would eat gluten-free pepperoni pizza together and watch our latest DVD series. "Plus," I reasoned, "I have a day to recover tomorrow since the kids will be in school and I have nothing else planned." A banal comfortable routine seemed like the height of luxury at that moment.

Just as I was saying this, the nurse brought another patient into the partitioned space next to me. Although I couldn't see her because the curtain was closed, I was like an unwilling fly held captive on her wall. She was sobbing and telling her husband that she was tired of being opened up, tired of people seeing her butt, and she didn't want to wear the gown.

"What did I ever do to deserve cancer?" she cried. "I don't want to die—why do I have to die?"

Her husband murmured, "Honey, be reasonable; everything will be alright; no I've never thought much about death; don't say stupid things, I won't stand for it; everything will be alright."

I met the outpouring of her heart with mixed feelings. I felt, first and foremost, a determination to bravely face whatever I needed to go through—not just that day, but whatever I came up against in the future. Crying and balking couldn't change the situation, even if I had done much of that myself.

Then I felt an overwhelming compassion for what she was going through—how frightened and trapped she felt. Since social protocol dictated that I couldn't pull the curtain aside to speak comforting words to her, I just prayed. I prayed she would be healed from her cancer and that she would be relieved of her intense anxiety. Even though I had been there for six hours already, they took her before me, and I was content. The poor woman needed to get through her anxiety-inducing procedure as soon as possible.

Eventually I was wheeled to the operating "block" as they called it. I balanced my body on the narrow table under the great white light, and the doctors stretched my arms out on either side of me and attached them to the support beams as if to a cross. An IV the size of a drinking straw was inserted in my hand, and I was told to think of something happy. I remembered our trip to Florida when Juliet was only six months old and Matthieu told me he was ready to move back to France. Just as I was about to go under, I quickly thought of other memories with my sons because I didn't want to fall asleep without thinking of them as well.

When I woke up, I was disoriented and cold. All around me were patients in various comatose states and I went in and out of awareness, though the bustle penetrated my groggy senses. The doctor took some time before coming to me, but when she finally made her way over, she told me the procedure had been a success. They were able to remove everything.

"But," I heard her say, "there was too much bleeding to see anything properly so you will have to come back for a hysteroscopy in one month's time to see if everything was removed." This procedure would be done without anesthesia.

At this point I was strung up on survival, determined to see the entire procedure through without complaining. I was disappointed, but I didn't feel it. I was angry, but I was too numb to care. When I moved my legs a little on the gurney, I noticed the ache inside—the invasion. It felt like I had been violated and I didn't know what to do with that feeling either.

By the time they wheeled me back to the room where Matthieu was waiting, I knew I had developed a fever before my temperature was taken because I felt burning hot and shaky. I was unsurprised when the nurse read, "101.5."

"They don't let you out of the hospital if you have a fever after surgery," I told Matthieu as I surrendered to the idea of staying the night. I battled to keep everything in perspective.

But Matthieu prayed I would be able to go home with him that night. Without being able to explain how it happened, I could tell my fever had left me before the nurse came back with the doctor. They were both surprised when my normal temperature was confirmed, but they saw no reason to keep me, so I was released and we went home together.

As we were driving home, I reflected that there would be no pepperoni pizza for me that night. The doctors had put a tube down my throat during the operation and it still hurt so much I could barely swallow. Then my mother-in-law arrived with the children ten minutes after we did, and I found out we had sent them to her house the night before with lice. *Agh.* Since we had no shampoo to treat them, we had to keep them home from school the next day.

So with the looming hysteroscopy, I had no closure. With the lump in my throat, I had no pizza. With the children home from school, I had no rest. As with everything else surrounding this pregnancy, nothing was turning out at all like I had planned.

In spite of everything, I was filled with contentment the next day. I was up and about, doing activities with the children and chores around the house. I don't know if it was remembering the patient who was my neighbor for that short hour, or if it was the fact that I just really appreciated the routine comfort of my life after all the uncertainty. Perhaps I had been able to find some closure after all.

A month later I had the hysteroscopy, which was not as painful as I had feared. But they found something abnormal and needed to take a sample. When I went back to get the results a few weeks later, the doctor examined the X-ray and shook her head.

"We didn't get everything out," she said. "You're going to need another D&C."

Before I could despair, she brought the results over to a colleague's office to confer, and his opinion was, "No, there's barely anything there. What are you going to do? Remove a few microscopic cells?" So my doctor considered the case closed. I was finally released from the prison of healing. I was finally free.

After wrenching myself from the physical aspects of recovery, I still had to deal with the emotional tentacles of grief, which were strangling my faith and joy. I started with the basics—an iron supplement after almost fainting at the grocery store. Then I decided to take an entire month's sabbatical from social activity to work through my anger, bitterness, and fatigue.

I had turned my face from God. I hadn't talked to Him since the day I found out Alistair was gone. Months went on like that until there came a point when I had no more physical distractions in my life. There came a point when I missed Him, when I lowered my boxing gloves and actually *talked* to Him.

"God, let's face it. I am really mad at you, and I have trouble believing, after everything you've done, that you care about me." I started to talk to Him like that, and I began to grieve more for my estranged relationship with Him than I did for my lost baby, although in that, I remained heartbroken.

During this time, my dear friend Lesley, whose husband had held together the ministry in New York when we went through the church upheaval, e-mailed me words of friendship and support. I wrote her back saying I had no idea how to overcome the bitterness I felt against God, and any insight she had to offer me would be welcome. Her simple heartfelt reply, full of compassion for my soul-aching sadness, was to remind me of a scripture in Lamentations that I didn't remember having read before.

For men are not cast off by the Lord forever. Though He brings grief, He will show compassion, so great is His unfailing love. For He does not willingly bring affliction or grief to the children of men.

As I meditated on this, a memory I had not thought about in many years came flooding back. When I first become a Christian, I regretted that I had not known this God earlier, this God worth changing my life for, because that meant my brother was lost—he had no chance. There had been no one to prove to him how much God loved him, the way I had learned through the scriptures.

I kept thinking, *if I had been there, I could have done something. I could have told him how much he was worth so he would never, ever take his own life.* I couldn't understand why God didn't bring me to him sooner, and I subconsciously blamed Him.

A year or two later, I was musing over this, and I had a vision. It was not a dream because I was awake, but I could see the whole scene clearly in my mind. I saw my brother Mark, sitting on the middle of the bed as the morning light streamed in through the half-closed blinds. He had the shotgun propped up in front of him, the bottom of the gun next to his foot, and the end of it in his mouth. He was teetering on the edge; he was about to make the decision to end his life.

Suddenly, I noticed he was not alone. There, sitting on the bed next to him, was Jesus. I could see his human form, but I recognized his holiness. As I registered His presence, I saw that He was crying.

It was in that moment—when I saw Him weeping over Mark's decision—that I understood that God gives us the choice to do what we want with our lives. He gives us the choice to take up our life or to leave it—to choose Him or to reject Him. But He doesn't remain insensible to what we choose. He weeps when we are pulled astray. He weeps when we suffer. He weeps when we end our life.

God does not *willingly* bring affliction or grief to the children of men.

God allowed Alistair to be taken away from me in accordance with His perfect will. His answer was not "yes" to what I so desperately wanted, it was "no"—and for reasons I cannot understand. But there had been so many times when He said "yes."

Yes! I will give men in exchange for your life. Yes! I will give you the desires of your heart. Yes! I will set you in a family. Yes! I will crown you with love and compassion. Yes! I will lead you with cords of human kindness. Yes! Nothing will separate you from the love that is in Christ Jesus. Yes! Yes! Yes! Mixed with these yeses, He gave me one crushing, heartbreaking no. It seemed unfair to accuse Him for that one time.

I was finally ready to call a truce. I had once believed a scripture about carrying a healthy baby to term and assumed that it was the one that applied to me. But this time, there was no such personal exultation over what I would receive. Instead, I was faced with a scripture that promised God's goodness.

My simple, heartfelt response to a scripture I had never remembered reading before was that I believed it. I believed that God would not willingly watch me suffer and remain unmoved. I believed in His goodness.

This was a promise I could hold on to. This was a promise that was meant for me.

I pray that out of his glorious riches he may strengthen you with power through his Spirit in your inner being, so that Christ may dwell in your hearts through faith. And I pray that you, being rooted and established in love, may have power, together with all the saints, to grasp how wide and long and high and deep is the love of Christ, and to know this love that surpasses knowledge—that you may be filled to the measure of all the fullness of God. Now to him who is able to do immeasurably more than all we ask or imagine, according to his power that is at work within us, to him be glory in the church and in Christ Jesus throughout all generations, for ever and ever! Amen.
Ephesians 3

26

MY CUP OVERFLOWS

It's Sunday in June. The roses over the well are still blooming, and the hedge of lavender along the wall of the vegetable garden is blooming too. We're having house church today. It's held once a month, always with the same group that we've become close friends with, and we always meet at our place. We like hosting, and we have a big enough garden for everyone's children to play in.

We got a text from our Algerian friend, Mohand, who cannot come. His message said that he has a wedding to attend at noon, so in the absence of spiritual nourishment, he will be having couscous. This makes us laugh.

Hisil is in France working for Renault, but he has gone back to India for a week, so his wife Jobby is coming by train with her three children. There's Patrick, a Frenchman, whose wife has left for her summer vacation in Indonesia with the children. There's Francine and Rado, and Rado's sister Magalie, who will be heading back to Madagascar soon. We even have a couple visiting from San Francisco.

The sister from San Francisco sees what I'm pouring for Communion and pulls me to the side to ask about the wine. I assure her that it's alcohol-free because I have a CR background. She tells me that both of them do too, which pleases me—not for their sakes, but for mine.

Addiction is not talked about in France, which can feel lonely, and it's nice to be able to share with people who can relate.

I go on to tell her that I had to convince the church to use alcohol-free wine for Communion to protect those who struggled with addiction. To the quiet murmurs of, "Are you really that weak?" I had to defend my case, bringing up 1 Corinthians 8—that the exercise of freedom should not be used as a stumbling block to the weak. It was decided that Matthieu and I would talk about it openly for the Communion message at church one Sunday, and I would speak about my past.

Except, to my great embarrassment, I could barely get a coherent word out through my sobs. I felt humiliated to talk about it to people who couldn't really relate to me, or so it seemed. I was afraid they would look down on me for my weakness. But my vulnerability ended up freeing some who were quietly struggling in this area. A few people came up to Matthieu and me to talk about alcohol addiction and to ask for help. With the issue of dependency out in the open, the church began using alcohol-free wine for communion.

For our little house church, Matthieu speaks in English, giving a short message in the form of a discussion, while I sit translating for Francine and Rado in French. The English speakers outnumber the French speakers today. We sing a few hymns and then get up and bustle about getting lunch ready.

Francine made a large bowl of Cantonese rice, I made a sweet Thai coconut curry chicken, and Jobby brought a salty tomato curry with boiled eggs. We are such an ethnic mix—the only thing French is the baguette—and everything tastes so good together.

We serve the children first, and I watch with pleasure as my three follow the example of Jobby's children and eat their rice and sauce with their fingers. One day we will visit their family in India, now that we are close friends, and our children will do well to learn to fit in to the customs. In fact, let them be children of the world, ready to go anywhere and find their place in it. Nothing could suit their parents more.

Now the adults sit around the table eating, translating back and forth and telling stories of how we met our spouses. Not surprisingly, the stories are diverse. Jobby and Hisil had an arranged marriage by the church, approved of by their parents, but secretly agreed upon by themselves first. Rado fell in love at first sight with Francine and pursued her for a long time, but she thought he was too old for her. Friendship, definitely. Romance, no way. The way she says it, rolling her eyes, makes us laugh.

The couple from San Francisco has an interesting story too. She is Mexican and he is American. Years earlier they had both been dating other people, and by a strange coincidence, those other people happened to be brother and sister. So although they definitely knew who the other was, they didn't necessarily hear positive things. Fast forward some time and they were set up by mutual friends to go on a date, which they agreed to with some trepidation. Neither of them spoke the other's language, yet there was something there that caused them each to cross the border and visit the other faithfully for over a year, before finally agreeing to get married. The alignment of their paths makes everyone's eyes light up with interest, as does the story I tell of how I met Matthieu.

We go outside to take pictures next to the well since the San Franciscan couple are only passing through and want to have a memory of their visit. Our motley group is framed by the cheerful red roses, twisted into an arc on the trellis above our heads. At their request, I show the couple what's growing in our garden and how the plants are arranged. The kiwi vine is starting to weave its way through the wooden arch that leads to the vegetable garden, the strawberries are nearing the end of their season on one side, and the raspberries are beginning to ripen on the other.

We have split the expanse of earth into two levels, sowing grass where the wooden boxes hold green beans and carrots, and where, not far off, there is the peach tree that we planted in memory of Alistair. To our surprise, it's loaded with peaches in its first year.

At the back of the garden is a small picket border protecting the lettuce, and a wooden swing-set climbing with grapevines. The grapes are still so tiny they look like a fetus version of the cluster they will one day be. On the other side of the walkway are the potatoes that are almost in bloom and ready to dig up; there is the wooden clothesline that we put up with the thyme, mint, and sage planted underneath to lend fragrance to the freshly laundered clothes. Next to the strawberries are zucchini, and small pumpkins to make soup, come autumn. The garden is much prettier and greener than it was at the beginning when we tried to turn it into a farm, with rows of vegetables that would quickly get overrun with weeds.

Our guests leave about mid-afternoon, and we are left to ourselves. It's so beautiful outside, but I go indoors instead and sit at the piano we inherited. It's beautifully built, from 1870, with heavy scrolled handles on either side, and it retains its rich timbre of sound. The tall windows are open, and the one overlooking the garden is filled with the large green leaves of the linden tree that shades our patio. Everything feels right today.

This is a rare moment of peace for me. The depression and anxiety I first recognized as a child, which have claimed a permanent residence in my psyche for as long as I can remember, are more familiar to me than peace. The demons, which were louder before becoming a Christian, nevertheless continue to haunt me and cause me to doubt my worth. Although I've trained myself over the years to keep from spiraling into despair, this state of mind is the one I naturally fall back on—my default view of the world.

If there is any area in which I can claim to be wiser, it is that I now recognize the war. I've learned that the enemy is not found in the outward attacks, like the grief over my brother's suicide or the deaths in Africa. It is not in alcoholism, or miscarriage, or the car accident that landed me with head trauma and depression. These are not the things that threaten to destroy me. On the contrary, they make me stronger. No—the war is in my own mind where the demons are always crouching at the door of my thoughts, waiting to accuse, to bewilder, to devour.

There's the whisper that tells me how important appearances are, and how much I fall short. In two weeks it will be my baby's due date, or what would have been his due date, and shortly after that we leave for Brittany. While this vacation is always filled with simple family pleasures, it is there, more than anywhere else, that I feel ashamed at having been unable to take off excess weight, exposed as I am in my beach garb. If there had been a new baby, I would have had an excuse. But now my arms are empty, and my quota for shame is full. In this area, I'm tempted to believe I am worth nothing, and to believe it so acutely it's paralyzing.

There is the demon of doubt that would have me believe I am not a success. I doubt how well I am carrying out my most important charge—to raise my children—and doubt whether they will turn out okay. There is no question that they are warm, well-fed, and loved, but too often my anxiety wraps me in isolation, and I fear for how it affects them. *And you wanted one more*, I accuse myself.

The worst is the demon of self-loathing, which drowns me in accusations about how I should not have done this or said that. Sometimes it feels like life rips away at my soul, like hyenas worrying at a carcass, snarling and tearing it to pieces.

There are the thoughts I cannot keep at bay where I struggle so much with self-accusation and self-loathing, the only relief I feel comes when I imagine stabbing myself repeatedly in the chest. Lately, I have been shoving Jesus between the knife and me—or He has been jumping in on his own—and that takes away a little of the enthusiasm in my self-immolation. My mind believes it's not true, but my reflex for imagining self-harm takes over and brings about calm, much like the effects of a drug. This imagery is something I fight on a daily basis.

Here in France, I am well placed to forge a new way of thinking—new positive paths of thought that will one day become more deeply grooved than the old. I'm only forty-two, after all, and have another half a lifetime to live, should I be so blessed.

One prevalent strength of French women is their capacity to care for themselves. I hear and see it all around me—women carving out time to do yoga or have a leisurely meal or get their hair done. They even go to the grocery store well-dressed because they believe they're worth putting their best foot forward at every moment. Though I am still a foreigner in many ways, I am learning. In some ways, I am becoming a French woman too. Slowly.

My physical therapist listens to me talk and stress about losing weight or not being good enough. Finally she exclaims, *"Faîtes vous plaisir,"* in playful reproach. The literal translation is, "Give yourself pleasure," and if you could remove the sexual connotation it would be perfect. "Enjoy life." "Treat yourself." "Live it up."

"You're going through life with your hand brake on," she tells me, which strikes me as a powerful analogy since I had actually done that a few times when I first started to drive. When I hear that, I can almost perceive what she's saying. I can almost envision a new way of viewing life, a new way of being.

I suspect these demons will always follow me, hound me, try to corner me to where I can hear no voice but theirs; but I will not be overrun. I remember the first scripture I ever learned from the Bible as a child. If anyone knows any verse from the Bible, it is this one: Psalm 23.

> *The Lord is my shepherd, I lack nothing.*
> *He makes me lie down in green pastures,*
> *He leads me beside quiet waters,*
> *He restores my soul.*
> *He guides me along the right paths for His name's sake.*
> *Even though I walk through the valley of the shadow of death,*
> *I will fear no evil, for You are with me;*
> *Your rod and Your staff, they comfort me.*
> *You prepare a table before me in the presence of my enemies.*
> *You anoint my head with oil; my cup overflows.*
> *Surely Your goodness and mercy will follow me all the days of my life,*
> *and I will dwell in the house of the Lord forever.*

This scripture still speaks to me, though it's now familiar and worn. It tugs at me simply because I know what the valley of the shadow of death looks like; I have walked through it several times. And I have always made it to the other side.

There is this paradox we live in where nothing on this earth is promised, and yet blessing upon blessing pour out of the heavens so that the storehouses of our hearts cannot even contain them. There is this God who is terrifying and distant and holy, yet He is so close and maternal He longs to gather us under His wings; He weeps over our suffering and parts the heavens to come down and rescue us. There is the indisputable fact that in this life we will have many troubles, and yet I *know* I need not fear evil, for God is with me. It is a truth I have witnessed first-hand. Trying to embrace this dichotomy is about as natural as a small child clomping around the room in his father's shoes, which are ten sizes too big.

My daughter summed it up in guided innocence, as only a child can, when she prayed over a particular heartbreak one evening, caused by her parents' refusal to witness the theatre piece she and her friends had put together at ten o'clock at night when it was just time for the guests to go home. She prayed, "God thank you for this—not so great day. Thank you for joy; thank you for sadness. Thank you for You, the King of Kings, the Lord of Lords. Thank you for Jesus, dying on the cross. And thank you for my parents, even though they are sometimes annoying—"

Matthieu started to laugh.

"What?" she asked in mock exasperation. "I know sometimes we kids are annoying, but sometimes you parents are too." Then she concluded, "In Jesus' name I pray."

In her youth, my daughter is still so illuminated by innocence she can thank God for joy and sadness in the same breath. She can honor her God, even when she finds her parents incredibly frustrating. She is filled with all the wonder of who God is. The fact that she can also experience sadness in His presence does not seem paradoxical to her at all.

These troubles we have, sometimes large and terrifying, sometimes pesky and distracting, are bound to come. But they don't have to shake our footing. I have this grateful confidence that goodness and mercy will surely follow me all the days of my life, and that when the race is run, I will have crossed the finish line. The demons may whisper that I am not worth as much as anyone else, but they cannot remove the fact that I am worth dying for.

So my trust is not in my worth, but in the nature of God and His eternal presence.

It is because of this confidence that I can echo my daughter's prayer —not in guided innocence, but in conscious faith. I might be reduced to my knees, my head bowed low perhaps, but it is with an indomitable spirit flung towards the heavens that I pray—

Thank you for joy, my Father.
Thank you for sadness.
Thank you for my life, even when the battle is at its fiercest.
Thank you for you—the King of Kings, the Lord of Lords.
And thank you for Jesus dying on the cross.
Amen and Amen.

EPILOGUE

It's nice to know how things have continued with an author after you've immersed yourself in the memories of twenty years of her life, isn't it?

In the years since I wrote *Stars Upside Down*, my life has, unsurprisingly, evolved. My children have grown. I have one teenager, another kid who can't wait to be one, and a third who is happy to stay young because that's where the imaginary world dwells. The peach tree we planted for Alistair has sadly not survived, and we'll have to dig it up this year. Had I known peach trees were so fragile, I would have chosen another fruit. We continue to remember Alistair in other ways.

I am more comfortable in my own skin as I age, and I no longer suffer from doubts regarding my self worth. Two years ago, I went off antidepressants after twenty years of taking them. It's not always easy. I struggle with anxiety and maintaining a cheerful outlook on life, but so far I am managing through more natural methods. We still meet as a house church at our place once a month. And although the Indians have gone back to Chennai, taking with them their three children and culinary contributions, they have since visited us, and we also stayed with them in India last Christmas where our kids picked up as if they had never left off. Otherwise, we have begun attending the pre-teen and teen camps in Switzerland each summer with the larger community of French-speaking churches, whom we've grown to love. The Swiss Alps are ridiculously beautiful if ever you get a chance to go.

As for the rest, I continue to write posts on faith and French life on my blog, *A Lady in France*, and I now write clean romance books, with a focus on the Regency era.

I continue to love and admire the goodness and beauty that is all around us—the gift to creation from a magnificent God. What a splendid world we live in, wouldn't you say?

A LETTER TO MY READERS

First, I want to thank you. Thank you for reading my words and accompanying me on my journey.

You may have noticed, that in my endeavor for authenticity, I sometimes portrayed God how I perceived Him at the time, not how He actually is. I want to make it clear that when I said things like, "God was nowhere to be found," I am not making a statement about God, but rather about the condition of my faith in that moment. And when I said, "After all, He was the one who took my baby away," I was writing of my feelings during that period—much like a psalmist— and not attempting to throw a shadow on a holy God.

I tried to keep everything true to how it happened according to my memory. Of course, memory can sometimes be faulty. All the events and people are real, though in some cases, I've changed their names for privacy or to avoid confusion. Let me put in a disclaimer for poor Olivier (not his real name). I made him out to be a jerk, but he was really just young and not the right guy for me.

Some people have wondered about what church I attend. I purposefully left it out of the memoir because I wanted the focus to be where it should—on God, and not on my church. However, it's no secret, so I'll share with you here that I am part of the International

Churches of Christ and am currently worshipping with the ministry in Paris.

Leaving a review on Amazon (and Goodreads if you are there) is a great way to support authors. It keeps the book more visible in the searches and lets other readers find out what kind of book it is. If you liked the book and want to support me in that way—even a one-line review will help—you will be doing me a great kindness. You can leave a review. If you're also motivated to spread the word on Facebook, why, let me just give you the biggest virtual hug imaginable.

For those thinking of using *Stars Upside Down* for a book club read, I might be able to join in via Skype if you wish it. If you'd like to contact me for book club, speaking, or other reasons, you can reach me at *aladyinfrance@gmail.com*. I always try to respond.

Want to know what else I'm working on? You can sign up for my newsletter by checking out my author site, *jenniegoutet.com*. I update it each time a new release comes out. You can also read my blog, *aladyinfrance.com*, where I write about French recipes, the Bible, and my life.

Stay tuned for my next release, a pure Regency romance called *A Regrettable Proposal*, which will be published by Cedar Fort in March 2019.

Jennie

ACKNOWLEDGMENTS

My husband gets my first word of love and appreciation. You believed in me, and even created a writing studio for me, so I could work uninterruptedly. I love your humor, strength, godliness, wisdom, and dancing feet. To borrow from our days in New York—you are da bomb.

Juliet, Gabriel, and William, I love each of you so much, and so differently. Don't think for a minute that because I suffered from postpartum depression that you were not, and are not, everything desired, special, perfect, and marvelous in my eyes. Thank you for being patient while I worked, and for giving me something to live for.

I had some amazing early supporters. Julie—how you could have seen through the skeleton of a draft I handed you to tell me I had something good, I don't know. But I think if you had been anything but completely encouraging, I wouldn't have shown this book to anyone else, and it would have died an early death. Thank you. This book is here because of you.

Thank you Rosalind, for hosting us in New York and for reading through my second draft with such a fine attention to detail, not to mention giving me such excellent pointers. You are a gem.

Lesley, you told me I could do better, and you told me how to do it, and for that I love you. Without you, I'm not sure I would have found my voice.

Rachel, thank you for all your wise advice on my manuscript. And thank you for showing up at Mark's funeral, an act of love that still touches me twenty years later.

Lizzie Harwood, thank you for the heart you put into editing my book. It was so refreshing to be edited by someone who cared about what I wrote, and it really boosted me as a first-time author.

Emily Moliné, I will never look at my writing in the same way again without wondering what other superfluous phrase I can cut. Working with you has been illuminating, and I mean that as the highest praise.

Lacey O'Connor, I'm lucky to have found you. Thank you for your ceaseless drafts of cover design and interior layout in your tireless quest to find what suits me.

Thanks to my Mom and Dad for raising us so well, and to Ned and Treese for being such an important part of their (and our) lives. Stephanie, you always have my back, and Jeff, you are still flawless in my eyes. Mark, I wish you were not gone.

Neyra, Sue, and Lisa—thank you for buying my wedding dress and for teaching me what it meant to be family before I had one of my own.

For my blog supporters who read the memoir as it came out, chapter by chapter, thank you. Alison, you were always the first to read and leave me comments and I heart you (and I can't forget Tracie and Andrea—the list goes on). Stacey, you overlooked the faith aspect and loved my book and me anyway.

Finally, let me give a big, hands-in-the-air shout of gratitude to my Father in heaven—who always deserves the last word.

ABOUT THE AUTHOR

Photo credit: Caroline Aoustin

Jennie Goutet is author of the award-winning memoir, *Stars Upside Down*, the Regency novel, *A Regrettable Proposal*, and the modern romance, *A Noble Affair*. She is a contributing author to *Sunshine After the Storm*, and *That's Paris - an Anthology of Love, Life and Sarcasm in Paris*. She was a BlogHer Voice of the Year pick three times, and her writing has appeared on Huffington Post, Queen Latifah's website, Mamalode, BonBonBreak, and BlogHer. Jennie has lived in Asia, Africa, Europe and Manhattan, and she weaves these cultural flavors into her stories. A Christian, a cook, a reader of classics, and an inveterate klutz, she lives with her husband and three children in a small town outside Paris and writes about it on her blog, aladyinfrance.com. You can learn more about Jennie and her books on her author website, jenniegoutet.com, or by following her on twitter, FB, Instagram, and Pinterest.

Made in the USA
Middletown, DE
06 January 2019